THE EVE OF ST. MARK

*"Until the dusk eve left her dark
Upon the legend of St. Mark."*

THE EVE OF ST. MARK

A Play in Two Acts

By
MAXWELL ANDERSON

ANDERSON HOUSE
Washington, D.C.
1942

NOTE

GEORGE BANTA PUBLISHING COMPANY, MENASHA, WISCONSIN

Dedicated to Sergeant Lee Chambers—

    one of the first to go, one of the first to die
    that we may keep this earth for free men.

CHARACTERS

DECKMAN WEST
CY
NELL WEST
ZIP WEST
RALPH WEST
NEIL WEST
PETE FELLER
JANET FELLER
PRIVATE QUIZZ WEST
CORPORAL TATE
PRIVATE THOMAS MULVE-
    ROY

PRIVATE SHEVLIN
PRIVATE FRANCIS MARION
PRIVATE BUSCEMI
SERGEANT RUBY
LILL BIRD
SAL BIRD
A WAITER
FLASH
DIMPLES
SERGEANT KRIVEN
PEPE

ACT I

1. Nell West's kitchen, April, '41
2. The barracks at Fort Grace
3. Janet's room
4. The Moonbow Restaurant
5. Nell's kitchen, September, '41

ACT II

1. A pier
2. A field, October, '41
3. The cave on the island, April, '42
4. Nell's room
5. Janet's room
6. The island
7. The kitchen, June, '42

THE EVE OF ST. MARK

ACT ONE

Act One

SCENE: A background of curtains, against which is set the furniture of a farm kitchen. A white-enamelled range at stage left. In the center a leaf-table covered with light oil-cloth. To the right a kitchen cabinet. There are seven or eight chairs around or near the table.

DECKMAN WEST *and his wife,* NELL, *both about forty-five, have been eating the post-chores breakfast. Two sons,* NEIL, *eighteen, and* ZIP, *sixteen, are lingering at the table with them.* CY, *a lean old neighbor of fifty or so, is finishing a huge plate of boiled potatoes. His way with a potato is to cut it into chunks, then butter and eat one chunk at a time. It's early April, 1941.*

Deck. How's that creek road?

Cy. Under a certain amount of water. The snow's melting down the south slope and the waves was breaking right under the wagon box.

[*He looks at the dish of potatoes.*]

If I had it to do over again I'd go back and come by boat.

Deck. The table's yours, Cy. We're all through.

Cy. Maybe you wondered a little why I didn't eat breakfast at home. Well, the truth is I'm here to report I've lost my wife and children.

Nell. Lost them? What do you mean?

Cy. B'gob, they left me.

Nell. Where have they gone?

Cy. Off down the road in a county car.

Nell. You mean, the county took the children?

Cy. Welfare took 'em, Deck, wife and kids both. Come to find out, she asked for it. She complained the windows was broke out in the upper story and the boys wasn't getting vitamins. Which was true.

Deck. You know, not to speak out plain or anything, if your farm got run down it was her doing. You got to have a woman on a farm, or it won't pay, and that one you had wouldn't hardly classify as a woman.

Cy. I kinda liked her, and I'm gonta miss the little shavers, but looks like I'm a bachelor from now on.—I was wondering if you needed a hired man, with a good team of loggin' horses and a natural affinity for manure.

Deck. We could certainly use you, Cy, with Quizz in the army and these two in school most of the time. I don't know what mother'd say.

Nell. Well—I've been cooking for a kitchen full since I was twenty, and I may as well keep on.

Deck. I don't know.

Cy. Plate of potatoes three times a day and sleep in the barn.

Neil. You don't have to put up a sales talk, Cy. We know you're good.

Zip. He's certainly good at snakin' logs. He can pile those big maples like toothpicks.

Cy. Tell you what I'll do. I'll go out and help around the barn. Any time you can get along without me, you toss out my blanket. Coming along, boys?

[*He starts to go.*]

Neil. Sure.

Deck. All right, Cy.
[CY *and the* BOYS *go out.*]

Nell. I really should get up and make myself start the dishes.

Deck.
[*Putting an arm around her*]
What's the matter, mother?

Nell. Nothing, I guess. I don't know.

Deck. You don't want him here, do you?

Nell. I guess it's—I kept thinking that I'd have to see him across the table instead of Quizz. Maybe for years.

Deck. We'll tell him to try further on.

Nell. Oh no, Deck. I was just thinking about Quizz and his coming today, that's all.

Deck. Where'd you put that letter?

Nell. On the side-board. I know it by heart if you want to hear it.

Deck. I want to look at it.
[*He gets the letter and sits down.*]
"I don't know how much time I'll have, but I'll see you, and that'll be good. And I'll have a chance to show you the most wonderful person in the world."

Nell. He can't be married.

Deck. No. She must be coming with him.

Nell. She'd better be beautiful.

Deck. Can you understand it, mother—our being grown up

and having grown up children, old enough to wear a uniform?

Nell. No. I just can't understand it.

Deck. And I can't. Doggone it, I go rushing around here, buying hay and selling hay and suddenly I'm an old man and my son's fighting a war.

Nell. Yes.

Deck. And I keep wondering about us when we were twenty. Did we look as young as that?

Nell. I wonder.

Deck. And why did I have to have a funny little girl with glasses? There I was, a dashing young Lothario, come of a family of dashing young Lotharios, the pick of the town at my feet, writhing for mercy, and what do I do? I pick me a funny little girl with glasses that didn't care whether I came or stayed.

Nell. I never understood that either.

Deck. Well, it's too late to change now. All those beautiful girls are grandmothers now.

Nell.

   [*Affectionately*]

I'm not a grandmother yet, remember.

Deck. You could be. Quizz is twenty-two.

Nell. Yes, but I don't think I am. And you're not a grandfather. But the war does rush everything. It sort of crowds us toward the exit.

Deck. I guess that's what it is. There's a car in the yard. Might be Peter.

Nell. It's past time for the mail.

> [RALPH *enters, Deck's brother, two or three years older, with graying hair. A tall, dreamy farmer.*]

Deck. Morning, Ralph.

Ralph. Morning, Deck. Morning, Nell.

Nell. Back from the creamery already?

Ralph. Well, Nell, it's getting so I drive in more to pass the time of day than to haul milk. If gasoline and milk cost the same I'd break even, but prices being the way they are I lose money on the trip.

> [*To* DECK]

I picked up your freight receipts at the depot. The Pennsylvania Railroad claims that hay'll leave for the metropolis Tuesday morning.

Deck. Tuesday? I'm going to quit shipping out of Ischua.

Ralph. The only thing to do with that town's cut around it with a hay knife and sink it.

> [*He goes to the door.*]

I just ran across a son of yours down the road. Wearing a kind of khaki colored suit of clothes.

Nell. Really? Where was he?

Ralph. Sitting on the porch at Feller's. I offered him a hitch this way, but he had some particular business and said he'd be right along.

Nell. I'd better call the Feller's.

Ralph. Phone's out again this morning.

Deck. What's the matter with it?

Ralph. I don't know unless old lady Boon burnt a connection with what she said over it last night. She called me up to speak about the telephone bill, and I told her the contraption was out of order half the time so I intended to pay half rates. She lit into me plenty hot, and I said, "Ma Boon, if you get too sassy I'll chop this line loose from my woodshed and it'll fall right back in your lap." She was about to respond, but just that minute the wire went dead. I guess she thinks I took the axe to it.

Deck. Half the time when there's a telegram for me she forgets to call me up, and I find out about it just late enough to lose a customer.

Nell. But how did Quizz get out from town?

Ralph. I gather Pete was picking up the mail at the station. So he gave him a ride up.

Deck. Probably coming along the ridge now.
　　[*He steps out.*]

Nell. How's Ethel?

Ralph. Oh, she's pretty docile. Give me another thirty years and I'll break her in to being a farmer's wife. Some days, when the weather ain't bad, she comes pretty close to being affectionate. It just goes to show a woman can get used to anything.
　　[PETE FELLER *enters with a handful of mail which he takes to the table.*]

Feller. Hello, Nell. Nothing to sign. How you standing it, Ralph?

Ralph. Dwindling, Pete, dwindling.
　　[JANET FELLER, *a neighbor girl, comes in with a package of yarn, lingering behind her father.*]

Nell. Oh, Janet, thanks. That's the yarn, isn't it? You didn't need to carry it.

Janet. I just rode up with dad. I'll walk back.

Nell. Didn't Quizz come? Were you joking, Ralph?

Ralph.
[*Going toward the door*]
He's out there now, looking like a leftenant.

Feller. Yeah, I brought your military man along with the mail. Be right in.
[RALPH *and* FELLER *go out together.*]

Janet. He's just getting a bag out of the car.
[NELL *sits, looking toward the entrance.*]
It's hard to get khaki now. They let me have enough for one sweater.

Nell. Well, I'll knit one at a time, anyway. Sit down, Janet.

Janet. I guess I won't stay. I—
[*She turns toward the door.* DECK *comes in carrying* QUIZZ'S *bag.* QUIZZ, *wearing a soldier's uniform, follows him.*]

Quizz. Hello, mother. Don't get up, please.
[*He crosses and puts his arms round* NELL.]
And everything's just the way it was. Mother and dad and the hill, and everything. I never thought I'd climb that old hill again!

Nell. Why, son?

Quizz. It just seems like another world, there in the camp. Not the same world.

Nell. Was it hard to get away?

Quizz. Well, kind of. You never know what's going on, and you can't find out. Oh, Janet! I want to—

Janet. I'd better run home now. I have some things—

Quizz. Oh, no, you won't. Oh, no.

Janet. Yes, please. I'd much rather.

Quizz. Look, Janet—there's only one of me—and I've only got one day. I don't want to waste it traveling up and down a dirt road. You stay here.

Nell.

[*Rising, beginning to suspect*]

Why, Quizz!

Deck. Doggone it, mother, you can leave it to Quizz to keep things neat and handy. He's picked himself a neighbor girl. I was wondering when some bright boy would notice there was a pretty girl at the Feller's.

Nell. More than one's noticed that.

Janet. Please, Mrs. West.

[*She wants to go.*]

Quizz. Oh, come on, Janet. Stand still long enough so we can get this straightened out.

Nell. I thought you meant you were bringing someone—

Quizz. No, what I said was I wanted to show you the most wonderful person in the world. It was kind of a surprise when she turned out to be a next hill neighbor. But there it was—and there she is.

Deck. That's one of the prettiest blushes I ever saw on a face, darling, so you step right out and show it.

Nell. Yes, Janet—don't hide away in a corner—

Janet. I'm sorry.

[*But she stays where she is.*]

Quizz. I've got a lot of things to explain all at once—so maybe I'd better start right in. I just managed to wangle this one day. I'm supposed to be on my way to Fort Grace, you see, but I was able to prove to the old man

I'd get there sooner by coming a little out of my way, so I can be here till five o'clock.

Nell. Oh.

Quizz. Yes, just till five, mother.

Deck. I must say your soldier clothes become you, son.

Quizz. That's how I managed to waylay Janet. It's the uniform does it.

Nell. But where in the world did you see Janet?

Quizz. Ah—trust mother to put her finger on it. That's the funny thing. That's the thing you'll never believe, because I don't believe it myself. I was at Camp Upton, mother, and when I got my first day off I went to New York, naturally. There was nothing much to do in New York, not for a jeep with no money, so I took in Rockefeller Center.—There was a guide showing a whole crowd of us around, and when we got to the tower—

Janet. Quizz—

Quizz. Yes?

Janet. Don't tell it. Please.

Quizz. Why not?

Janet. I don't know. I just don't want you to tell it.

Quizz. Well, that's the whole point of the story. It's the whole point of everything. Everything up to now.

Janet. No. No, please. You mustn't, Quizz. Nobody knows about that. Nobody can ever know it.

Quizz. Listen, darling, I don't know what you mean. Dad and mother—they naturally—they said where in the world did we meet.—Well, there's nothing wrong with it, only it was completely unbelievable—that's all—so why not tell them?

Janet. I never dreamed you'd tell anybody.—I—to save my life I wouldn't tell anybody. And you can't—

Quizz. Well, look, Janet—you're making it seem as if we had something to hide. There's nothing wrong with the way we met. It was fun, and it was certainly unusual, but—you see, I was standing beside this girl in the tower. I'd been watching her all along, and then when I found myself standing beside her I said the first thing that came into my head. I said, "You're the most beautiful person I've ever seen in my life."

Janet. I'll never forgive you! Never!
[*She rushes out.*]

Nell. What's the matter?
[*She rises.*]

Quizz. I've no idea. I didn't want to hurt anybody's feelings.—Well, I'll finish it anyway.—I said, "You're the most beautiful person I've ever seen in my life," and I meant it. And she looked at me very pleasant and cool and said, "Thank you." And I said, "After this barker gets through barking maybe we could have a little lunch together." And she looked me all up and down and looked at my uniform and said, "Yes, that would be very nice, thank you." Well, I thought she looked a little familiar, but she was so blossomed out and beautiful it wasn't till we were half way through lunch that I found out she was little Janet Feller that lived two miles away from here. And she didn't know who I was till I told her. Then— we had the afternoon and evening together—and—then we seemed to feel the same way—so—

Deck. How'd she get to Radio City?

Quizz. Won a contest. Maybe that's what she doesn't want me to tell. It was some silly business for high school girls in domestic economy classes. She baked the best cake with a certain kind of flour, and that was the prize, the trip to Radio City.

Nell. Oh, I heard about it—that Janet won.

Deck. I'll just step in and see if she's through crying.
[*He follows* JANET.]

Quizz. Do you like her, mother?

Nell. You couldn't have done better, Quizz. She's sweet.

Quizz. And you'll forgive me for not coming straight home— and for maybe—not spending much time here—

Nell. You'd be a poor specimen if you hung around your mother much today, I guess.

Quizz. But—I love you. Just as much. And I've never forgotten what you said to me.

Nell. I'm not very wise, son.

Quizz. You're wise enough to tell me.

Nell. Some things we think we've learned, just by living, Deck and I, and one of them is—that's the best part of life—loving somebody and being true. I think she'll always love you.

Quizz. So do I. And it makes me—
[*He crosses and kisses* NELL.]

Never mind. You know what it does to me.

Nell. It's made me rich all my life.
[DECK *comes out of the inner room with his arm around* JANET.]

Deck. I've been telling Janet, mother, that we've always wanted a girl. We have these three omadhauns of boys, and they damn near wore us out with their racket and their flying around.—But what we wanted was a daughter to smooth things out, and now we've got one.

Quizz. I didn't want to hurt you, Janet. I just thought we might as well tell it the way it was.

Nell. Maybe Janet thought it sounded a little as if you'd picked her up—and she didn't like that.

Quizz. Personally I like the way it happened. What's a pick-up, anyway? It's love at first sight. So why not say it the way it was?

Janet. But you couldn't say it the way it was—because you had no idea what was happening.
  [*She still stands with Deck's arm around her.*]

Quizz. I was there, wasn't I?

Janet. Yes—but you were looking at the buildings.

Quizz. What did you see that I didn't?

Janet. If you're going to be really honest and tell it—then I have to tell my side, too. You see, I knew who you were. From the beginning.

Quizz. You brat—you said you didn't.

Janet. I know.

Quizz. Well, what of it?

Janet. And I went and stood beside you on the tower. Because I—because you were from out here—and I—

Quizz. You were lonely.

Janet. No.—You see—I knew if you told this I'd have to tell it all—and—. You see, I knew who you were, the minute I saw your shoulders—and I'd have known you anywhere. It seems to me—all my life I'd have known you anywhere. You never saw me at all, but I knew every time your car passed the house. And then you didn't even know me. And I had to go and stand beside you to make you notice me.

Quizz. You little devil! But I was noticing you.

Nell. Darling, our Quizz is going to be away a long time from the looks of things, and you and I are both going to be lonely. It's true—what Deck said about our wanting a daughter. Will you come up once in a while—when Quizz is gone—come over often as you can—and bring his letters?

Janet. Yes, of course.

Nell. Because I think he'll write to you more than to us—and we'll want to know where he is.

Janet. I'll come.

Nell. And now there's only part of a day left—so you take your arm from around that slim waist, Deck, and turn her over to Quizz.

Deck. I get a kiss first.

    [JANET *kisses* DECK. *He releases her.*]

Nell. If you're hungry or anything, come and see us, but it's your day, what there is left of it.

Quizz. We thought we'd walk back to Janet's house and—sort of explore around. Maybe down to the cemetery meadow. The whole country seems new to us—because we never saw it together.

Deck. The road's a bit sloppy for walking, and the wind's raw, blowing off the snow. I know it's spring according to the calendar.

Quizz. It certainly seems like spring to me.—Doesn't it, Janet?

Janet. Yes, it does.

Deck. I guess when you're young you can smell it earlier.

Quizz. So we won't mind walking.

Nell. Then off you go. And it's spring.
[QUIZZ *and* JANET *turn toward the door.* NEIL *and* ZIP *enter.*]

Neil. Well, what do you know! It's a soldier!

Zip. I gathered there was somebody important here!
[*They surround* QUIZZ.]
Boy, you look like Napoleon!

Quizz. Hello, Neil. Hello, Zip. Hell, you're almost big enough for the army yourself.

Zip. Almost. You know what we're doing today? We're taking time out to inspect our big brother.

Quizz. No school?

Neil. Not when Quizz gets home on leave.

Zip. You know what we thought? We thought maybe we ought to climb up and look at the maples. The sap's running like a brook and Ralph says his syrup's thick enough to fill a tooth.

Neil. We thought we'd like to candy a little on a snow-drift, the way we used to.

Quizz. I certainly would like to—

Nell. You boys run along and let Quizz take a walk with Janet. They're starting back toward her house together.

Zip. With—

Neil. Hello, Janet.

Janet. Hello.

Zip. What's going on here?

Deck. Good God, they can take a walk, can't they?

Quizz. Mind you, we'll be back. We'll see you later.

Neil. Sure.

Quizz. So long.

Zip. So long, General.

Janet. Goodbye.
[QUIZZ *and* JANET *go out.*]

Zip. What the hell is going on here?

Deck. Looks a little to an old man like they was fixing to get engaged.

Zip. Yeah. I see.

Neil. I could run them down in Old Faithful.

Nell. They want to walk.
[NEIL *and* ZIP *appear to be looking out a window.*]

Zip. In all that slush?

Nell. That's right.

Zip. Looks like we lost the best brother we ever had.

Neil. Looks that way.

CURTAIN

Act One

SCENE: Six army cots set in two rows lengthwise to the audience as in an army barracks, and against the same background of curtains.

Quizz sits on a bunk at the left rear, writing a letter on a pad which he holds on his knee. Three other soldiers, Cor-poral Tate, Private Mulveroy and Private Shevlin are rolling dice against a cardboard placed beside a cot.

April, 1941.

Tate. Head him off, somebody! He's rolling all sevens!

Mulveroy. Bite 'em, ivories, bite 'em for papa's dinner! Seven!

Tate. Wait a minute!

Shevlin. That's right. Seven.

Tate. I'm clean. That busts me.

[*He gets up to move away.*]

Mulveroy. Come on. Roll a couple more.

Shevlin. We gonto bump heads? That's no pleasure.

Mulveroy. Want to come in?

Quizz. The way I work it out I've got just enough to buy cigarettes and stamps and get my pants pressed.

Mulveroy. You mean you figured that all out?

Quizz. I had to.

Mulveroy. You got to get over that, soldier. That destroys ambition. That eliminates the element of chance. You're in the army for a whole year, remember! You gotta re-organize, gotta get on army time!

Tate. Stay away from him, Quizz. He's on the beam tonight. He can't miss. He'll rob you.

Quizz. I'm staying out.

Mulveroy.
[*To* TATE]

Hey, what do you mean, sorehead? You won yesterday, didn't you? I never yet tried to swindle a deal but you started queering the customers! You drive a man underground!

Tate. O.K. You go underground and stay there!

Mulveroy. You mean this game's going to languish because there's a guy won't risk his money? That ain't life in the army, see? Life in the army is like this—you get paid a little dab every so often. You take that little dab to a crap game and you either lose it or you run it up to something worth while. That's the way you live here! That's the rhythm! You got to get in the rhythm! Come on, run it up to something big enough to spend.

Quizz. O.K. I don't want to break an Irishman's heart.
[*He starts to rise, but at that moment* PRIVATE FRANCIS MARION *enters. He is a handsome Southerner.*]

Mulveroy
[*Turning on* MARION]

Oh, boy! Bat hides! He gives out bat hides! Come to me arms, Francis!

Tate. Wow! He's in! Pay me! Pay me!

Shevlin. Me first, Swamp Fox! Me first!

Marion.
[*With poise*]

Gentlemen, I greet you.

Mulveroy. Did you get paid?

Marion. I did.

Mulveroy. Where is it?
[MARION *produces a small roll of bills.*]

Tate. How much?

Marion. Allowing for the usual deductions, you ruffians will share among you the sum of twenty-two dollars and fourteen cents.

Shevlin. Where's the fourteen cents?

Marion. Forgive me. I bought a package of cigarettes.

Shevlin. You shouldn't do that. Not without permission.

Tate.
[*As they share the money*]

Hey, I rate a ten! I rate a ten! I only got two dollars last time!

Shevlin. You do not!

Tate. He owes me a month's pay, and I only get two dollars! Where's the justice in that?

Mulveroy. That'll teach you to grab quicker next time.
[*They count their money.*]

Quizz. What is this? A gang?

Marion. No, suh, this is my holding company, a perfectly legal arrangement. To tide me over one crisis after another these gentlemen have lent me money—

Shevlin. Not if I had it to do over again—

Marion. And finding that my total borrowings had grown to

an enormous sum, they organized to administer my affairs
—also to prevent any addition to the list of my creditors.
They are now a closed corporation, dedicated to supply-
ing my modest needs and collecting my monthly honor-
arium. You, for example, could not extend me credit. They
wouldn't allow it.

Quizz. Why that's terrible. That's restraint of trade.

Marion. It's an inconvenience.

> [PRIVATE BUSCEMI *enters, puts away his overseas cap and
> Springfield.*]

Quizz. How much is that enormous sum you owe?

Marion. Corporal Tate keeps the books, I believe.

Tate. The total was ninety-seven dollars before you came
in the door.

Quizz. You mean you were able to borrow ninety-seven dollars against your thirty a month?

Marion. People trust me no end. It's my accent does it.

Mulveroy. Hell, no, it was those ancestral estates in Marion
County which I'm beginning to doubt there is any such
county now.

Marion. Mulveroy is the cynic of the enterprise. He refuses
to believe that I am descended on my father's side from
Francis Marion and on my mother's side from Patrick
Henry. He refuses to believe that only three aunts, two
uncles, seven cousins and a grandfather stand between me
and my inheritance.

Quizz. Is there any truth in it?

Marion. The strangest thing about it is it's all true.

Quizz. Then why in time did you have to borrow money?

Shevlin. Because he drinks like a fish, that's why.

Marion. You see, at heart I'm a very sorrowful fellow, and when my sorrow mounts to a certain point, I must drink.

Tate. Also he drinks Cuba Libras, and they're expensive.

Marion. But in the end I pay. You saw me in the act of paying.

Buscemi. Wait a minute! I'm a member! Where's mine?

Marion.
> [*With dignity*]
> Yes, you Yankee pirates, you carpet-bagging sons-of-bitches, Private Buscemi is a member in good standing! Where's his share?
> [*He goes to his bunk and gets out a clean shirt.*]

Shevlin. If Mulveroy'll let go of three dollars I'll do the same.

Mulveroy.
> [*Shrieking*]
> Three dollars?

Shevlin. That's right.

Mulveroy. O.K.
> [*Together they pay* BUSCEMI *six dollars.*]

Buscemi. Anybody going anywhere tonight?

Mulveroy. We're all going except dead men.

Tate. I've got to wait here for Sergeant Ruby. He said something about appointing me Charge of Quarters.
> [*The rest begin to get ready to go out.*]

Mulveroy. That's right, you're a corporal now. We got to watch this censored son of a censoring censor from now on. He's joined the government.

Tate. Can I help it if I'm brighter than you are?

Mulveroy. Now he's talking about his I.Q. I saw you fooling with those little puzzles, Corporal. You didn't do so good, I guess.

Tate. I got 'em all across the river without eating each other, and that's better'n you did, soldier.—I don't know what happened to Ruby. He said he'd be here at seven and it's half-past.

Buscemi. He's down at the mess-hall. All the tops are being lectured by a couple of staff officers down there.

Tate. What are they getting lectured about?

Shevlin. What do you care? We'll get it all from Ruby to-morrow.

Buscemi. You won't get what I heard. I was standing guard right outside the window. There's a sprout up in front with charts and figures and he's discussing sexual inter-course.

Mulveroy. Did he know about it?

Buscemi. He's got a theory about it. He says they made a study and he's got it all down in percentages. Twenty per cent of the men in an army camp will refuse all tempta-tions to sexual intercourse because they've got wives or sweethearts and so they don't want to play. And then another twenty per cent will take anything they can get. You know, the way it is with you, Mulveroy.

Mulveroy. They got to have shoes. I draw the line there. They got to go home and get their shoes.

Buscemi. But then he goes on and says, there's sixty per cent in between that maybe will and maybe won't depending on the temptation.

Tate. The loot said that?

Buscemi. That's what he said.

Shevlin. I don't know why he's talking to the non-coms. They all belong to that lower twenty per cent.

Buscemi. And he's got a project, the loot. He wants all the non-coms to help him. Look, he says, there's twenty per cent that don't need any help. And there's twenty per cent you can't do anything with. But the big sixty per cent in between, there we can exert an influence, he says. There we can save a lot of boys from contamination. And if you ask me how, he says, there's only one way—offer them something better.

[*A pause*]

Marion. For instance?

Buscemi. That's where the guard came to relieve me. I never did hear what they're going to offer.

Shevlin. Now there's perfidy for you. Sergeant Ruby comes out of a highly moral lecture like that and makes for Amityville and a rendezvous with Lill and Sal.

Tate. Who's Lill and Sal?

Shevlin. I don't know. All I know is I heard a little phone conversation through the wall up there, and Sergeant Ruby and Sergeant Kriven are meeting Lill and Sal at the Moonbow at eight o'clock.

Buscemi. Not the way that lecture's holding out they won't. Mulveroy, do you know any Lill and Sal?

Mulveroy. Wait a minute. Sure. They're twins. They live on Charlotte Street. Tourists and paying guests. They've got an old mother to support. Last name's Bird.

Marion. Are they virtuous?

Mulveroy. Wait a minute. I just remembered. I don't know why I've been passing them up lately. I used to have a home there. They're wonderful. I think I'll get there ahead of the Sergeant.

[*He begins to hurry.*]

Buscemi.

[*To* MARION]

No. Not virtuous.

Mulveroy. By God, I'm going there. Sergeant Ruby can't take my home from me. They're much too good for that goon.

Quizz. Sergeant Ruby appears to be unpopular around here.

Mulveroy.

[*Shrieking*]

Sergeant Ruby? You don't know him yet. Wait till he tears into you!

[*He begins to imitate Ruby's enunciation which sounds like Brooklynese dragged through all the slums of the world.*]

'Tenshun! Fall in! Give ta boy a taste of what he's gonna get! Get ta hell on your feet and take ta position of a soldier! Don't you know ta position of a soldier, ya dumb bunny?

[*They all line up except* TATE *and* QUIZZ.]

Pull in at pod!

[*He walks up and down in front of them, addressing remarks as he stops before each one.*]

Inspection! Arms! Look, you! We're doing Inspection Arms!

[SERGEANT RUBY *enters behind* MULVEROY. *The others try discreetly to pipe* MULVEROY *down. He grows more raucous.* RUBY *stands waiting. He is an elderly rather stolid-looking old-line sergeant.*]

· 25 ·

At a Command Arms take a position a Port Arms! You hear?
Port Arms! Is dat a way to hold a gun? Gimme at gun!

[*He snatches an imaginary Springfield.*]

See dat! At's a way ta hold a gun! Take da gun!

[*He slams it back at* SHEVLIN, *half knocking him down.*]

Stand up! Stay on your feet when addressed by ya officer!
You heard me! Inspection! Arms! At a Command Arms take
ta position a Port Arms! Wit ta fingers of ta left hand
closed place ta left thumb on ta operating rod handle and
push ta handle to da rear—What ta hell you tink you're
doing there?—to da rear! Da rear! till caught by operating
rod catch, at ta same time lower da head an' eyes sufficient
to glance in da receiver! Lower da God-dam head! Having
found ta receiver empty—

[*He stops, feeling a presence behind him, and turns round.
The line melts away. There is a pause.*]

I was just trying to give them an idea of Inspection Arms,
Sergeant.

Ruby. Ya Charge of Quarters tonight, Tate.

Tate. O.K., Sergeant.

[RUBY *crosses to go out, then pauses.*]

Tanks for ta ad. Yeah, tanks for ta ad.

Marion. I hope you won't take our little games too seriously,
Sergeant Ruby. The psychologists say that a certain
amount of irreverence and disrespect is healthy in the
armed forces, and should be encouraged.

Ruby. Yeah? Well, I don't know what it says in da books, but
when I see a smart, brainy squad like dis it gives me ideas,
see? It makes me tink of tings. Tings like poimanent K.P.,
and duty wit da foitilizer wagon, and latrine detail. It
makes me tink of yard duty special, and policing up, and
twenty-four hour guard duty and running the lengt of da

company street carrying da God-damn rifle over ya ruttin head. Dis whole ruttin squad is goin to have more ruttin fun dan you could write home about. I'm going ta take a poisonal interest in every ruttin one of you. Toin in an get ya ruttin sleep. Ya gonta need it.
[*He goes inside. There is a pause.*]

Shevlin. Now we're in good and deep. You're a genius, Mulveroy, just a blatting genius.

Buscemi. Couldn't you see us piping you down, you Irish maniac?

Mulveroy. Hell, do you want to be popular with the ruttin' non-coms? What are you bucking for? We got enough corporals around here! You better get the hell out of here, Corporal! You been kicked upstairs.

Tate. Yeah, I got to get my instructions. Well, so long, buddies; remember me in your Cuba Libras and any whoring you do.

Mulveroy. Get the hell out.

Tate. You're breaking my heart.
[*He goes inside.*]

Mulveroy. Listen!
[*A pause*]
Ruby's taking a shower. He can't catch that quarter-of bus. Let's go meet those guineas in the Moonbow.

Buscemi. How many do you want?

Mulveroy. The whole outfit.

Shevlin. Thanks. I've got my own little home.

Mulveroy. Come on, Buscemi. We can find more girls. Only don't try to take my sweetheart. Lill's my gal; you get Sal.
[*At the door*]

You coming, Marion?

Marion. I'm penniless, Dublin. I'm flat as a one-eyed jack.

Mulveroy. What's money? There's a drink in it; come on.
[*He goes out, followed by* BUSCEMI *and* SHEVLIN.]

Marion. You're not going?

Quizz. If I thought I could trust one of them to mail a letter—

Marion. I wouldn't advise it. Not a letter to a lady near and
dear.

Quizz. I'd better go then.
[*He gets his overseas cap and his letter.*]

Marion. I'll go with you.
[*He begins to get ready.*]

There's no great hurry. The bus stops across at the Hall,
and we'll see the lights coming down the street.
[*As he buttons his collar at the mirror*]

You haven't been talking much.

Quizz. I'm listening mostly, so far.

Marion. When you make up your mind about anything, let
me know. I'd be greatly obliged.

Quizz. I only know one thing. You can't run out on it. You
have to go along and do your damnedest.

Marion. What's the chance of us all being let out after our
year's up?

Quizz. Not a chance in the world.

Marion. That's what I think.

Quizz. Would you want to get out?

Marion. For myself, I have infinite natural gall, and great presence of mind, but I'm in a hell of a fog. I walk around and around in it, but I can't think it through.

Quizz. What's the problem?

Marian. Well, there's going to be a hell of a war, some of us are going to die young, and, the others are going to benefit by it. Which are the lucky ones? Which would I rather be?

Quizz. You'd rather be one that almost got killed and didn't.

Marion. Yes, but then another question arises. How close do I have to come to being horizontal before I earn the right to remain perpendicular?

Quizz. I don't know that.

Marion. I guess nobody knows or we'd have God damn well been told by this time.

Quizz. I know this much. I read the entire manual of arms coming down on the train, and it's not in there.

Marion. No. I looked for it there. I shall look for it tonight at the bottom of a coke with rum. That's the bus now.
  [*They run out.*]

CURTAIN

Act One

SCENE III

SCENE: Janet Feller's bed is set against the curtains in a splash of light. A small bed table with an oil lamp stands at its head. No other details of the room are visible.

JANET *sits on the edge of the bed in a robe, writing a letter in a tablet. She writes, then looks up, then writes again. Laying down the tablet, she thinks for a moment, then takes a khaki handkerchief out of the robe, unfolds it and smooths it on her knee. Her father calls from outside. She jumps guiltily.*

Feller.

[*Outside*]

Janet!

Janet.

[*Rising and thrusting the kerchief away*]

Yes, daddy.

Feller.

[*Outside*]

I'm going into town. Anything you want?

Janet. When are you going?

Feller.

[*Outside*]

Right away. So if you want a letter mailed or anything—

Janet. I'll have it ready in just a minute.

Feller.

[*Outside*]

And Janet?

Janet. Yes? Come in.

· 30 ·

Feller.
[*Entering*]
Charley Lane's boy's downstairs. Says he wants to see you.

Janet. I've told him not to come.

Feller. He's a pretty nice boy, and he drove over all the way from Port Allegheny, so I couldn't tell him to turn around and go home.

Janet. I don't want to see him. I told him not to come.

Feller. Shall I say you're going into town with me?

Janet. Will you, daddy?

Feller. Sure. And you can mail the letter yourself.

Janet. I'll just put on a dress.
[*She throws off the robe, slips two dresses from their hangers, chooses the dark one and puts it on. Then she takes a hasty glance in a little mirror, picks up the letter, opens it to kiss the end, stamps it, and starts to go. The handkerchief has fallen to the floor. She comes back for it, replaces it inside her dress and runs out.*]

CURTAIN

Act One

SCENE: One fairly large restaurant table set before the curtains. LILL and SAL are seated at it with a couple of drinks. MULVEROY, BUSCEMI and MARION have just come up and negotiations are in progress. LILL and SAL are both wearing a little too much of everything, but they are attractive.

Lill. Sure, you can sit down if you want to, Mr. Mulveroy, that is as far as I'm concerned you can sit down, but as far as Sal's concerned I can't speak for her, because we make a point of being entirely separate and distinct personalities.

Mulveroy. Look, Lill—
   [*He sits.*]

Lill. So as for her I can't decide, but I will say, Mr. Mulveroy, when a soldier comes in and sits down at a table a girl's got the privilege to say she was waiting for somebody else.

Mulveroy. You better let me sit beside you, girl, because you've been taking that one extra drink and you're getting elaborate for this early in the evening.

Lill. I am not elaborate! I'll murder anybody that says I'm elaborate! Was I, Sal?

Sal. Just a little, Lill, just a little.

Lill. Gee, was I? Maybe I was, at that.

Mulveroy. I been away, you know, and I certainly missed my little home.

Lill. You been working the other side of the street, big Irish, that's where you've been.

Mulveroy. I been walking up and down the whole world, kid, and I never found anybody I loved like Lill.

[*He whispers in her ear. She listens stonily.*]

Sal.

[*To* BUSCEMI]

You better ask your friend to sit down. You'll never get anywhere standing up in the middle of a restaurant.

Marion. I'll sit over here.

Sal. No, sit with us, soldier. There's safety in numbers.

[BUSCEMI *is next to* SAL. MARION *sits beside* BUSCEMI. *A* WAITER *goes through on flat feet.*]

Buscemi. Oh, waiter!

[*The* WAITER *disappears.*]

Sal. He'll see you by appointment only.

Lill.

[*To* MULVEROY]

All I can say is you certainly brought yourself back at an inconvenient occasion.

Mulveroy. And I know why it's inconvenient, too.

Lill. If you know why it's inconvenient, will you kindly go on the air with the information?

Mulveroy. I got back last night, see? I been a cadreman out at Fort Knox. And what's the first thing I hear? I hear Sergeant Ruby bragging he's going out tonight with Lill and Sergeant Kriven's going out with Sal. Now, mind you, if you like him better that's all right. Only I don't like the way he talks about you.

Lill. You're no cadreman. Was he ever a cadreman?

· 33 ·

Marion. Indeed he was a cadreman at Fort Knox, Miss Bird, and he has just returned.

Lill.
    [*To* MULVEROY]
You certainly got handsome friends. O.K. If you say it I believe it. What was Sergeant Ruby talking about?

Mulveroy. He was just explaining how he and Kriven had a technique that never failed yet, see? A technique for getting on some kind of time with girls.

Lill. What kind of time?

Mulveroy. War time.

Buscemi. And tonight they're going to use it on you.

Sal. Oh, you heard it, too?

Buscemi. Oh, sure, I heard it.

Sal. It's kind of touching the way they all tell the same lies, ain't it? Kind of like the three musketeers. Only it's going to be thick with sergeants around here in a few minutes. Maybe you-all'd better take cover.

Mulveroy. Why don't you cut away with us now?

Lill. Because I gave my word of honor we'd be here at eight o'clock, and that's all a poor girl's got. Just her word of honor, that's all.
    [*She takes a sip.*]
Just her word of honor.

Mulveroy. You better let me put one hand over that scamper-juice like I used to. You're getting elaborate and la-de-da.

Lill. I am not getting la-de-da! I'm simply saying—Sal, am I getting la-de-da?

Sal. You better let him put his hand over your drink.

Lill. O.K. You can put your hand over it. But it don't mean anything.

> [MULVEROY *shields her glass with one hand. The* WAITER *goes through again.*]

Mulveroy. Waiter! Waiter! We want three Cuba Libras and five hamburgers!

> [*The* WAITER *disappears.* MULVEROY *jumps up.*]

Hey, for God's sake, what is this?

> [*He yells after the* WAITER.]

You hear that? Three Cuba Libras and five hamburgers!

> [QUIZZ *comes in quietly and sits beside* MARION.]

Buscemi. Make mine well done with onions.

Mulveroy. Two of them well done with onions!

Sal. Make mine rare.

Lill. And mine.

Mulveroy.

> [*Yelling*]

Two rare! What are we talking about? Who are we talking to? Is this a restaurant? Why does that flat-foot go away and leave us?

> [*The* WAITER *returns.*]

Waiter. Hey, there's a couple M.P.'s up in front. You better button the flap.

Mulveroy. You're a liar; there's nobody up in front! There's nobody anywhere! This is the deep South and we're lost in it! We're all alone! Bring us four Cuba Libras and six hamburgers! We got another customer!

> [*The* WAITER *goes.*]

Sal. Get him out of here. We don't want to be caught on the downbeat.

Lill. You'll have to take off, Mr. Mulveroy. We're waiting for the sergeants.

Mulveroy. Oh, you're waiting for the Goodyear men. O.K., girl. We know what they think about you. We saw those two in the drug store tonight, buying medical supplies!

Lill. You did not!

Mulveroy. You got a low threshold for Goodyear sergeants!

Lill. I hate sergeants, and I hate you, and I hate the whole damn army! What did you have to come to this town for, anyway, with your whole army, spoiling everything! We didn't ask for you! We didn't want you here! We had everything nice, and we went to church on Sunday, and I could 'a got married, and then you come along with your army and it's all spoiled! I want it to be the way it was before you came along!

Mulveroy. Wait a minute! There was a sergeant before I came along!

Lill. There was not! I'll murder—He was going steady with me before you came long, and now what do I get? They want to have a drink and then they want to go out and look at the stars! Astronomy! Only they never see the stars! Oh, no! And I hate you all and the whole God-damn army and I want it to be the way it was!

Sal. You better quiet down, Lill, and all four of you scram.

Lill. That's the kind of boys there used to be, see?
    [*She indicates* MARION *and* QUIZZ.]

Quiet boys that respected you, like that one.

[*To* MARION]

You respect me, don't you?

Marion. Lady, your sentiments do honor to the women of the old South, and your conversation is fascinating.

Lill. You hear that? He can talk to a girl, and he don't have to drag in stars.

[*Two pretty girls,* FLASH *and* DIMPLES, *enter and cross toward the left.*]

Flash.

[*Pausing at the door*]

Oh, Thomas!

Mulveroy. Yeah?

Flash. Could I see you a minute?

Mulveroy. Hullo, Flash. Hullo, Dimples. Sure.

[*He converses apart with* FLASH.]

Sal. Thomas, huh?

Marion. Refined, you think?

Lill. And I mean refined.

Mulveroy. Oh, Buscemi?

Buscemi. Yeah?

Mulveroy. Come here a minute.

[BUSCEMI *joins* MULVEROY *and the* TWO GIRLS.]

Lill. I guess they had a little something to talk over.

Marion. He's their spiritual advisor. They come to him for guidance and religious instruction.

Lill. You hear that, Sal? Religious instruction.

· 37 ·

Sal. For the best instruction you got to get under a good teacher.

Lill. I wouldn't be surprised.

Mulveroy. Oh, Lill?

Lill. Yes, Thomas?

Mulveroy. We have to step out for a minute. See you later.

Lill. Not if I see you, Thomas.

Marion. He's going for a cadreman. An apostolic cadreman.
[*The* WAITER *enters with a tray, halting the quartet in the door.*]

Sal. Hey, who's paying for this?

Mulveroy.
[*Going out*]
Charge it to astronomy.

Quizz. I'll pay for it.
[MULVEROY, BUSCEMI *and the* Two GIRLS *go out.*]

Sal. What?

Quizz. I'll pay for it.

Sal. You know, I like this silent job here. When he speaks he says something. That's the first word he spoke, but, boy, did he make it count?
[*She lifts a glass.*]

Silent job, I love you. Come on, drink to the silent job, he's paying.
[*Her arm goes round* QUIZZ.]

Lill. It's nice to be quiet for a change.
[*She drinks.* MARION *empties his glass.*]

Sal. You don't like my arm around you, do you?

Quizz. Certainly I like your arm around me. What do you
think I'm made of?
[*He lifts his drink.*]

Sal. You're blushing.

Quizz. I do that for a come-on, you know. I start blushing,
and the girls say, look, he's bashful. And then they throw
their arms around me.

Sal. Look, the silent job can talk, and he's got a technique.

Quizz. Only thing bothers me, what do we do when the non-
coms walk in?

Sal. We'll tell 'em we're busy.

Quizz. Yeah, but that won't help tomorrow.

Lill. You afraid of non-coms?

Quizz. Lady, in civilian clothes, no, but in the army they've
got the drop on us.
[*The* WAITER *goes out.*]

Sal. They're late, you see, and you bought us a drink. A
soldier can finish his drink, can't he?
[MARION *helps himself to a full glass.*]

Lill. This handsome job of mine, he's reaching for drinks in
every direction.

Marion. Alcohol stimulates a love of the beautiful and the
good.

Lill. Is that me?

Marion. That's you.

Lill. Doesn't he talk like an angel? I'm through with that rough stuff—I honestly am.

Quizz. I guess this town was different before the army settled down here, wasn't it?

Sal. It certainly was. It was completely dead. It was nice, though. I liked it, didn't I, Lill?

Lill. It was certainly better than what we've got here now. This is practically inflation, what we've got now.

Quizz. What do you mean, inflation?

Lill. You know, kind of dizzy—like you put out your hand, and what have you got?

Quizz. A drink, probably.

Lill. Yeah, that's right, a drink.

Quizz. What was it like when you used to go to church?

Sal. We used to wear dresses just alike, Lill and me, and the usher took us up front so everybody could see us.

Quizz. That must have been something.

Lill. I used to love the organ. But that church is strictly a wreck now. The windows and everything. It used to be beautiful.

Marion. "Beautiful as a wreck of Paradise."

Lill. What's that?

Marion. It's a line from a valentine a civilian wrote long ago. "Beautiful as a wreck of Paradise."—I used to be a civilian myself. I had a cabin overlooking a lake, and I sat there reading Keats and Shelly and T. S. Eliot. Not a year ago. The copse was thrilled with bird song. Warblers.

> "And sang within the bloody wood
>   When Agamemnon cried aloud,
> And let their liquid droppings fall
>   To stain the stiff dishonored shroud."

Sal. What did you say about the cops being thrilled?

Marion. A copse is a little grove, a hidden virginal grove.

Lill. What was he doing for a living?

Quizz. He was waiting for his grandfather to die.

Lill. You don't say?

Marion. Three aunts, two uncles, seven cousins and a grand-father. "Long lingering out a young man's revenue."

Lill. Jesus, I'm falling in love.

Marion. I'll be unfaithful.

Lill. So will I.

Marion. Good. You have a generous heart.

Lill. Jesus.

Marion. It's the spring that does it. Spring, the sweet spring, when the meadows flush green and yellow, and the first pussy-willows show along the brook, and the milk begins to taste of onions.

Lill. Honest to God!
   [*She kisses* Marion.]

Sal. You know what's going to happen?

Quizz. What?

Sal. They're going to walk in here and take us away from you.

Quizz. You want to escape from these sergeants?

Sal. Sure we do.

Quizz. The rear booth's empty—the one with the curtains. Some people just came out of it. You and Lill could sit in the booth, and when Ruby arrives we'll say you waited and then went home.

Sal. You hear that, Lill?

Lill. Sure I heard it.

Sal. Will you do it?

Quizz. We certainly will.
    [*There is a noise to the left.*]

Sal. Who was that just came in?

Quizz.
    [*Looking*]
No, that's not Ruby. You've got time.

Sal. Will you give me a kiss, darling?

Quizz. Absolutely.
    [*He kisses her.*]

Sal. Tell me you love me.

Quizz. You want me to tell you the truth?

Sal. Sure I do.

Quizz. There's somebody else I love better.

Sal.
[*After a pause*]

That's all right. I don't mind. You'll—you'll forget about her when you know me. You'll forget her.

Quizz. Anything can happen.

Sal. That's it. Anything can happen.
[*She looks at the door.*]

Come on, Lill.

Lill. What was that poem you said?

Marion.

"The host with someone indistinct
　　Converses at the door, apart;
The nightingales are singing near
　　The Convent of the Sacred Heart.

"And sang within the bloody wood
　　When Agamemnon cried aloud,
And let their liquid droppings fall
　　To stain the stiff dishonored shroud."

Lill. It's the God damn poetry gets me! I don't know what it means!

Sal. Come on, come on. There's a crowd coming in.

Lill.
[*To* MARION]
Any time, baby, any time.

Marion. Yours till the dust-cart calls.
[LILL *and* SAL *go out.*]

Quizz. Are you interested?

Marion. They begin to verge on the professional, but I'm inclined to believe the whole of Amityville verges.

Quizz. There aren't enough girls.

Marion. Exactly. Of course, your situation may be different from mine. You mailed your letter.

Quizz. Did you have a letter to mail?

Marion.

> [*Taking a letter from his pocket*]

It's for the Wraith. She doesn't write to me. I write to her, but I don't mail the letters.

Quizz. What's the matter?

Marion. She doesn't answer.

Quizz. Where does she live?

Marion. St. Cloud, Minnesota.

Quizz. Oh, God.

Marion. Two thousand miles away, by road or rail.

Quizz. Is she beautiful?

Marion. Like a sunset.

Quizz. You're in love with her?

Marion. When I get no letter from her I lift an astral letter from the pile and pretend to read it. When I walk alone in the evening she walks beside me, her ectoplasm, her poltergeist walks beside me. I've got to exorcise her somehow. Are you in love?

Quizz. I mailed my letter.

Marion. What's she like?

Quizz. She lives on a farm. She's young.

Marion. Unsophisticated.

Quizz. As much so as they come nowadays.

Marion. Iseult is a dancer. Also she sings. She wants to go on the stage.

Quizz. How did you meet her?

Marion. In the old days—before the war. People used to flit up and down the country, you know. But now—distance is distance.

Quizz. You know what I think you ought to do?

Marion. I don't believe so.

Quizz. Mail that letter.

Marion. She won't answer.

Quizz. I think she will.

Marion. Why would she?

Quizz. She won't find anybody else that can quote verses to her.

Marion. I'm not sure she cares for verses any more.

Quizz. She'll answer this time.

Marion. Didn't we promise to love and cherish Lill and Sal?

Quizz. We promised to save them from worse than death, that's all.

Marion. Don't you have any hankering after the flesh-pots?

Quizz. Some. It's the drinks mostly.

Marion. I have a hell of a hankering.

Quizz. It won't kill you.

Marion. What if there's never anybody else, not even Lill and Sal? What if we never lie with anything warmer than the Pacific Ocean?

Quizz. You're maudlin.

Marion. On three free Cubas? No, no. I'm philosophic, delicately apprehensive. And I hanker. I definitely hanker.

Quizz. For those two flesh-pots.
  [SERGEANTS RUBY *and* KRIVEN *enter.* QUIZZ *rises.*]

Marion. One of them. Will you make a fourth?

Quizz. Oh, Sergeant Ruby, there was somebody looking for you.

Ruby. Yeah?

Quizz. A couple of girls, in fact. Named Lill and Sal. They said to say they waited as long as they could, and then went home.

Ruby. Dey did? Who da hell dey tink dey are?
  [*To* KRIVEN]
Dat's what comes a missin da bus, see?

Kriven. I guess we missed da bus, all right.

Ruby. So you hadda change da ruttin shirt—
  [RUBY *and* KRIVEN *go out.*]

Marion. Now what do we do?

Quizz. We take the bus back to camp and crawl into our own truckle beds.

Marion. I don't know as I like a man with that much character.

Quizz. It's not character. I just belong to the twenty per cent the loot was talking about.

Marion. Very well. You're the strong solid man, and you bear the purse. I bow to your judgment and follow. What am I, after all? The weakling scion of a decaying house. Do you mind if I put a sandwich in my pocket?

   [*He scoops one up.*]

Quizz. Finish the drinks if there's any left.

Marion. I will.

   [*He empties a glass.*]
   "So out went the candle and we were left darkling." Taps! Heel-taps. And thus the evening ends.

   [*They go out.*]

CURTAIN

Act One

*SCENE: The stage is arranged in two sections. On the left
the kitchen is set against the curtains more or less as before.
On the right Nell's bedroom, consisting only of a bed and a
chair or stand, takes up half the stage. When the curtain
rises the bedroom is dark, and only the kitchen is seen.*
DECK, NELL, NEIL, ZIP, JANET, RALPH *and* FELLER *are sitting or standing about listening to* QUIZZ.
September, 1941.

Quizz. I'd have had more time if I hadn't been so damn
lucky to start. You see, the battery commander gave me
three days, and said, "You better make the most of it. I
can't promise you any more." So I grabbed my extra shirt
and started for Amityville. Well, before the bus came
along, I got picked up by a fellow in a station wagon
that wanted me to help him drive. Sure I could help him
drive, and then, on the way into town, he told me he was
driving to Buffalo, New York, to deliver some pedigreed
sheep.

Zip. Buffalo?

Quizz. Yeah. Practically in our back yard. He had the sheep
in the back, a ram and five ewes. He wanted to drive all
night, and would I come along to spell with the driving?
Well, it was going to save me all that train fare, so I like a
fool took him up. Only that night after dinner he disappeared, and I had to hunt through every saloon in Harris-
burg before I could find him and get started. He was
pretty stinking, and I was going to quit and take the train
right there, but he gave me all his money to keep for him,
and the key to the car, so I thought it was going to be all
right. Anyway, I had to take care of the sheep. He didn't

even know enough to give 'em water. He didn't know there was any use for water any time. Well, the next night, right in Wellsville, he disappeared again. He didn't have a cent of money with him, but he stole two tires off his own station wagon and sold 'em to get drunk on. Well, I fed and watered the sheep and then I found him and gave him his money and the key to the car, and I took the next train. He can stay there and drink the rest of the tires and his pedigreed sheep, too. But I lost most of two days with that drip, and now I have to start back tonight.

Neil. No matter how much time you start out with it always whittles down to one afternoon.

Quizz. That's right.

Nell. Can't you be here this evening, Quizz?

Quizz. Just for dinner, mother. I'll have to take the ten o'clock in Olean. I'm sorry.

Nell. It's worse for you than for us.

Deck.
[*To* JANET]
Get out your camera, girl. Maybe he'll stand still long enough for a snap-shot.

Zip. Just a sucker for pedigreed sheep, that's all.

Quizz. God, I could have kicked myself all the way to Cattaraugus County—and I'd have made better time if I had.

Ralph. Have they let you fire a gun yet?

Quizz. I don't pull the lanyard. So far it's been my job to lug ammunition and cut the fuse before firing. We've got a good gun section. Anyway we got top rating in our battery.

Neil. That must be nervous work, cutting a fuse.

Quizz. The first time it scares you to death.

Deck. He always had a steady hand.
[Cy *comes in.*]

Cy. I don't want to hurry anybody, but if we don't get out there pretty soon there'll be another installment due on that baler, and no money to pay it with.

Nell. They'll be right out, Cy. They're just hanging around to embarrass Quizz and Janet.

Zip. Don't hurry the help, ma. I haven't finished my dessert yet.

Nell. Then you wade into it.

Deck. It's going to rain tonight, and we have to finish the cemetery meadow so we can move the rig.

Nell.
[*To* Quizz]
You two go in my room for a while if you want to talk. You'll never get rid of this gang.

Quizz. I guess we will, at that. We've got things to say.

Feller. You going to have dinner here, Janet?

Janet. I think I'd like to—if they want me.

Nell. Of course we want you.

Feller. I'll tell your mother. It'll be all right.

Quizz. Janet?

Janet. I'll help with the lunch dishes, Quizz.

Nell. No, no, Janet. Don't be exasperating. I don't want any help with the dishes.

> [JANET *and* QUIZZ *start to the right.*]

Zip. Don't you let him dictate to you, Janet. Make him promise you're to be the boss.

Cy. That's right. Because the way it starts out that's the way it's going to end.

Janet.

> [*Looking back at them*]

I—

Quizz. Don't pay any attention to them, Janet. They're just poking fun.

> [JANET *and* QUIZZ *go to the right.*]

Deck. Look, boys, you can't keep bankers' hours on a farm, not unless you want the bank to take it away from you.

> [*The lights go out on the kitchen and come up on the bedroom.* JANET *has sat on the chair.* QUIZZ *comes up to her and takes her hand.*]

Quizz. Come, sit beside me.

Janet.

> [*Holding back*]

Not yet. Couldn't we talk, just a little first?

Quizz.

> [*Sitting on the bed*]

Yes, of course. Only—it's so different from your letters.

Janet. So different?

Quizz. You said things in your letters—about wanting to see me.

Janet. Of course I did. Only when I see you again, after a long time, it always seems as if I don't know you at all. As if we had—almost to begin all over again.

Quizz. I hope not. Oh, God, I hope not.

Janet. No, no, not really—but—I have to look at you and hear your voice. I can't believe it's—

Quizz. What?

Janet. You see, you've been with—so many people—and you've done so many things I don't know about. It can't be—quite the same for you as it was. Is it just the same?

Quizz. Oh, darling—just more so, that's all. I've lain awake at night, whenever I wasn't too tired, just thinking about you—and all day, whenever I didn't have to think about something else, you'd slip into my mind, and I'd think about you. And your letters—how I loved you and thanked you for those letters.

Janet. I was always afraid they'd sound—

Quizz. They came—oh, they came like rain in a dry year, darling—and you can't imagine how dry—and how much I needed them.

Janet.
[*Her hand on her bosom*]
I carried yours here, all the time.

Quizz. You see?
[*He kneels at her feet, taking her hand, looking up at her.*]

Janet.
[*With a long breath*]
I—I just couldn't believe it was true.

Quizz. Couldn't I kiss you now?

Janet. I kept thinking there must be somebody else. Wasn't there anybody else?

Quizz. No. Nobody.

Janet. You see, one hears so many things—about the camps. The girls have brothers there—and it isn't like being at home, being in camp.

Quizz. No, God knows it isn't. And, I'll tell you the truth, Janet, if it hadn't been for you I could have got mixed up in all sorts of things. Because the things are there to get mixed up in. But, darling, I just used you for a north star and I steered straight for you as fast as I could come.

Janet. Yes, it's true.
[*She runs her hand over his hair.*]
Yes, you are Quizz, and you're not changed.—You didn't mind—what I said?

Quizz. No, sweet; you're right about it. It's—so different it's —well, I couldn't believe this farm was here—or you— or any of it. I'd feel your letter in my pocket some time when I was out on maneuvers or in a restaurant—or at chow—and I couldn't believe there was such a girl. You have to kind of hang on anyway.

Janet. Did you want to believe—?

Quizz. Did I want to believe—? A fellow hangs on to some-body the way he hangs on to life. God, I wish I could tell you.

Janet. You don't need to. I know now.
[*She leans over and kisses him.*]

Quizz. It's all right?

Janet. Yes.—I only wish we had more days.

Quizz. Those damn sheep.

Janet. Never mind. That was like you, too. Feeding them before you left.

Zip.
[*From the kitchen*]
Quizz?

Quizz. Yeah, Zip?

Zip. We're going. We could use another man on that baler, if you really want to come.

Quizz. I'll bet you could, at that.

Zip. It's going to rain tonight.

Quizz. I did my time in those fields, boy. It's your turn now.

Zip. O.K., General.
[*A door slams in the kitchen.*]

Janet. Do they really need you?

Quizz. No, no.

Janet. What did he mean then?

Quizz. He was just letting us know that the house was all ours.
[*He pulls her to her feet.*]
Sit beside me.

Janet. Your mother's in the kitchen.

Quizz. She went to the upper orchard for some apples. I saw her pass the window. Sit here.
[*They sit together on the bed. He puts an arm round her.*]
Will you kiss me now?

Janet. Yes.
> [*She kisses him. He holds her close.*]

Quizz. That's more like your letters.

Janet. I love you, Quizz.

Quizz. I love you, Janet.

Janet. I mean it forever when I say it. Forever and ever.

Quizz. I never meant less than forever, darling.
> [*Her arms tighten around him.*]

Janet. If we only had our own house.

Quizz. Yeah. The only house I have has one room, and there are fifty other fellows sleeping in it besides me. It makes the whole thing kind of awkward.

Janet. When will you get another furlough?

Quizz. I'm not expecting another till after—well, after whatever's coming.

Janet. After what?

Quizz. Well, we never know what the general staff's thinking, you know. But I gathered more or less we'd be getting on a train pretty soon.

Janet. A train?

Quizz. Probably for San Francisco. And points west.
> [*She straightens up.*]

Janet. And this is the last time—before you go?

Quizz. I think so.—You know, if anybody ever wished he had a house I'm wishing it now. A house for you and me.

Janet. There's no use being angry—and no use holding you back. Because you just have to go.

Quizz. I just have to go. And I think I should. I only wish it came a few days later.

Janet. I won't see you—till after—it's all over.

Quizz. I guess not.

Janet. What can I do? How can I live?

Quizz. Will you wait for me, Janet?

Janet. I'll have to wait for you.

Quizz. Janet?

Janet. Yes?

Quizz. Couldn't we—be together?

Janet. I—don't know.
   [*Her breath comes fast.*]
   I don't know anything about it.—We couldn't—be married?

Quizz. There wouldn't be time.

Janet. Suppose—there was a child. And we weren't married. And you never came back.

Quizz. I know.

Janet. You see, I don't know about it. What one does, so there won't be a child.

Quizz. I don't either.

Janet. Quizz, have you ever—?

Quizz. No, darling. You see, somebody told me—the way to

be happy—was to wait till you were in love—and I waited.

Janet. Who told you?

Quizz. My mother.

Janet. I want to be good to you.

Quizz. Kiss me.
[*They kiss.*]

Janet. But it couldn't be here.

Quizz. Why darling?

Janet. I don't know this house. It's not ours. No, no—I couldn't.

Quizz. There isn't any house for us, darling. I haven't any house.

Janet. But let's go somewhere. Not here.
[*The telephone rings in the kitchen—one long ring, two short.*]

Quizz. That's our ring.
[*He goes out toward the kitchen. She sits waiting.* Quizz *is heard answering in the kitchen.*]
Yes. Yes. Yes, Mrs. Boon. Yes, that's who it is. I see.—Will you say that again?—Before twelve?—Yes, I have it. Thanks.
[Quizz *returns.*]
There's been some mix-up. I have to be in camp before noon tomorrow. I can just catch the two o'clock train.

Janet. It's one now.

Quizz. Yes. You'll drive me. We'll have to hurry.

Janet. Oh, darling, darling—
   [*She runs to him.*]

Quizz.

   [*Kissing her quickly*]

Start the car, sweet. I'll get my things.
   [*They go into the kitchen, leaving the bedroom empty and lighted for a moment. The lights dim down quickly, then go out.*]

CURTAIN

THE EVE OF ST. MARK

ACT TWO

Act Two

*SCENE: A gangplank thrusts out from the wings in front
of the curtains to indicate a pier.*
RUBY, MARION, QUIZZ, TATE, MULVEROY, SHEVLIN *and*
BUSCEMI *wait at ease with overseas packs at the foot of the
gangplank. October, 1941.*

Tate. What's that noise?

Marion. That long withdrawing roar? That's the Pacific
Ocean beating at the Golden Gate.

Mulveroy. You mean you don't know the ocean when you
hear it?

Tate. How would I know? Closest I ever came to an ocean
was Lake Michigan.

Ruby. Ya gonna see ocean now. Boy, dis ruttin' ocean don't
never end. Last time I was in San Francisco we was
coming home from da Philippines. About a million men
came home 'at time, an' dey all got paid off at once. Tree
years' pay. Boy, was 'at a crap game? On ev'y ruttin'
ship dey played till one guy got all da paychecks. All
night, ev'y night, dey was playing, under da ruttin'
blankets wit' da candles. Den all a ships put in to Honolulu for a couple days, and da winners got togeder, and
den dey really run it up. Dey was about seven guys an'
about seven million dollars in dat Honolulu game and da
whole Goddam army was stony broke except dem seven.

Mulveroy. You didn't win?

Ruby. Me? I lost eleven hundred ruttin' smackers da foist
ruttin' day outa Manila. When I come to San Francisco
I couldn't buy cigarettes. We was all broke except tree

guys—a sergeant an' two udder soldiers. Dey went up Market Street wit a milatary guard, dose tree, each one taking about tree million dollars woit a paychecks to da National Bank. Jeez, wot a crap game!

Tate. Was gambling allowed back in those days?

Ruby. Soitanly not. It was strictly against da ruttin' regulations, same as now.

[KRIVEN *comes in from the left.*]

Kriven. Wot you guys waiting for?

Ruby. Dey moving some foiniture around to make room for us on da ruttin' boat. Dey's two tousan' men in dere already.

Kriven.

[*Turning*]

I'll be back in a couple of minutes. I gotta buy some medicine.

Quizz. Would you mail a letter, Sergeant?

Kriven. Where in hell would I mail a letter?

Quizz. I saw a box right outside the gate.

Kriven. Sure. Gimme da heifer dust.

[QUIZZ *hands the letter to* KRIVEN, *who goes out.*]

Tate. You know, it sort of sounds like a big ocean.

Marion. "Roll on, thou deep and dark blue ocean, roll!"

Ruby. Yeah, bo. Da ships rolled an' da ocean rolled, an' da dice rolled. Seven million bucks dem guys got.

[*A whistle blows from the ship.*]

A Voice. O.K., Sergeant!

Ruby. O.K., boys.

[*The soldiers begin to climb the gang-plank.*]

CURTAIN

Act Two

*SCENE: A field where the men are putting in winter rye.
A seeder stands at the left and several bags of seed grain are
piled at the right.* NELL *has carried out lunch for the men,
and* DECK *and* NELL *sit with* CY *while he finishes his lunch.
October, 1941.*

Nell. What will they do with your children?

Cy. Educate 'em, ma'am. Why, the welfare agent practically
promised me that one of 'em would be president, two of
'em senators, and the other two probably representatives.
He maintains it's all a matter of schoolin' and the glazing
in the upstairs windows.

Deck. They might surprise you, at that.

Cy. If he can train 'em into legislators I won't hold it against
him. But I don't expect no such reversal of form. I said
to him, "You can house a hop-toad in a canary cage," I
said, "and you can feed him on cuttle-bone and bird
seed—and maybe he'll eat a little of it before he'll starve,
but all hell can't make him sing." I said that and I left
him.

Deck. Aren't you kind of referring to yourself as a hop-
toad, Cy?

Cy. I ain't no canary.
[*He rises*]

Well, I guess the horses must have had their's by this time.
[*He turns to go*]

And here comes a pretty little messenger with the mail.

Nell. With the mail?
[*She rises*]

Cy. Quizz's girl.
[*He goes out.*]

Nell. It may be a letter.
[JANET *comes in.*]
A letter from him?

Janet.
[*Handing the mail to* NELL]
Yes. From San Francisco.

Nell.
[*Looking through the mail*]
None for us?

Janet. No, I didn't see one for you. And I haven't had time to read all of mine—I came right over with my father. But I knew you'd want to hear what news there was.

Deck. Sit down, girlie—and if you haven't read it all maybe you'd better glance through and skim those kisses off.

Janet. Yes, I will.
[*She sits to look at the letter.* NEIL *and* ZIP *come in.*]

Neil. Anything in the mail?

Deck. Janet has a letter.

Zip. Good news?

Janet. It's—from San Francisco.

Zip.
[*Looking at the mail, throwing it down*]
I lost interest in gun catalogues.

Neil.
[*Picking up the catalogue*]
Yeah?

Zip. Uncle Sam's got the shooting-irons nowadays. You can't buy anything out of a catalogue but a twenty-two—and that's a pop-gun.

Janet. I'll read as far as I've gone—this is to all of you.

[*She reads from the letter.*]

"Tell mother and dad and the boys I haven't had time for much writing. We've been on the way from one place to another mostly, or trying to catch some shut-eye. And tell mother and the others I was sorry not to say good-bye or eat that dinner that was in the oven. Several times since I've wished I had a dinner like that handy. It's a good thing I caught the train, though. I'd have been A.W.O.L. otherwise."

[*She pauses and looks up.*]

That's as far as I read.—

Deck. Go on, girl. You can stop when it gets personal.

Janet.

[*Reading*]

"I always wanted to see San Francisco and it's right here if I had a chance to look at it. I can say this much, they certainly have pretty water and pretty bridges here. The Golden Gate is really gold when the sun sets down the Pacific. But I keep thinking it's going to be high noon for you when it's midnight for me if we go where I think we're going. We'll be about as far apart as two people can be and stay on the earth. It certainly feels lonesome to think that."

[*She looks up.*]

Zip. That's all right, Janet. You just hurdle the love-stuff and go right on.

Janet.

[*Reading*]

"You remember I told you about Sergeant Ruby? Well, he's not so bad when you get to know him. He's served all over the world, Brooklyn, Haiti and San Diego and the Philippines, and he talks like all of them. "Sure ting I had a goil when I went out dere," he says. "But when I come back ta goil's married. So what? You're a soldier, so you go get you anoder goil." Only you've got to wait for me, darling. I don't know how to say it the way I want you to hear it, but you've got to wait for me."

[*She stops, reads a little, then goes on.*]

"Maybe you think it's funny I'd talk about you to the Sergeant, but I couldn't help it. Everybody knows all about everybody else here. Who your girl is and what she looks like and whether you've got more than one. You can't keep anything to yourself. And after a while you don't even try. So they all know about you—and now I'm rather glad they know, because I can talk about you sometimes—and that helps.—Oh, darling, if we'd only had—"

[*She stops again, reading on to herself.*]

Deck. All right, sweetheart. I guess the rest's up to you, and we'll let you off now.—Come on, boys, we're wasting farm labor.

[DECK *and the* BOYS *get up and move toward the left.*]

Neil. He gets it on paper. It sounds like Quizz.

Zip. It makes you realize he's a long way off, though. Doesn't it, Janet?

Janet.

[*Folding her letter*]

Yes.

Neil. We're going your way with the wagon, Janet, if you want to ride.

Janet. Yes, I'll go with you.

> [*The men go.* JANET *runs over to Nell, who takes her hands silently.* JANET *turns quickly, runs out.* NELL *puts the dishes in the lunch basket and goes toward the house.*]

CURTAIN

Act Two

SCENE: *Before the same curtains some empty cartridge cases, a few army blankets, a canteen or two, a stack of guns and miscellaneous equipment are placed to represent a corner of an ammunition dump hollowed from the rock of a Philippine Island. Those who leave or enter bow low as if through the entrance to a cave.*

MULVEROY *lies asleep under a blanket near left center. A* FILIPINO GIRL *sits watching him, a water gourd in her hand. A cannon booms miles away. From outside come the commands for loading and firing an artillery piece.*
April, 1942.

[*Before the curtain rises*]

Ruby.

[*Outside*]

Instrument direction, left nine five; time two two; three seven zero; base deflection, left one zero seven; converge at six zero zero zero; on number one open one zero; shell mark I; charge V; fuze long; battery, one round; zone seven; quadrant three one three; three two seven.

[*As curtain goes up*]

Tate.

[*Outside*]

Base deflection left one zero seven; on number one open seven; number one adjust; six three five zero; corrector five zero; charge V; time two two; number one, one round; three seven zero; fire.

[*A howitzer fires near the mouth of the cave.*]

Battery adjust; right five. Fire at will.

[*The howitzer fires three times at slow intervals.* SHEVLIN *and* MARION *come in from the right, cross to the left, pick*

*up a full cartridge case and carry it out to the right. As they
go toward the entrance* SHEVLIN *speaks to the native girl.*]

Shevlin. How's the big boy?

Girl. Mabuhti.

Shevlin. Attagirl.

[*To* MARION]

You're going to go down again before long. You're shaking.

Marion. I know. I begin to feel chilly around the edges.

[*They go out to the right, carrying the cartridge case.* QUIZZ
and BUSCEMI *enter and cross in the same fashion.*]

Buscemi. You know what you guys did today? You got all
three of those gun emplacements. I could see 'em from
the look-out. They're a wreck.

Quizz. We noticed the shells quit coming over in the afternoon. But the last one got Lieutenant Siegel, and the field
kitchen and the pharmacist's chest. And the pharmacist.

Buscemi. Must have got the quartermaster's, too.

Quizz. What there was left of it.

[*They go out to the left, then re-enter carrying a case.*]

Ruby's crawling around down there trying to find the
quinine tablets. He tastes everything he picks up, and if
it's bitter he puts it in the bottle.

[*They go out to the right.* MULVEROY *sits up and looks at
the girl. She offers him water. He stares at her and lies down
again, looking at the ceiling. The howitzer is fired again.*]

Mulveroy. What's that?

Girl. They fire the gun.

Mulveroy. What was that about quinine?

[*She shakes her head.*]

How long have I been here?

[*She raises three fingers.*]

Three days. And you've been sitting here all the time, for God's sake. You know, I've been out. I've been strictly out.

[*He sits up and looks at her.*]

I've been out so far I can't remember your name. That's the truth. That's what malaria does to you. What's your name?

Girl. You say Pepe.

Mulveroy. That's right. Peppy. What day is it?

[*She shakes her head.*]

No, you wouldn't know.

[*The gun is fired.*]

Somebody must have been taking my place in the section.—Listen, Peppy, you been away from your home three nights now. Your maman will raise hell. You better go home pronto. Will you go home now?

[*She shakes her head.*]

I'll tell you how it is, Peppy. I'm no good for you.

[*He sits up to talk to her.*]

You stick around me for a while and nobody'll marry you —and I won't marry you and you'll be a Goddamn social outcast. So you better go home.

Pepe.

[*Laying a hand on his forehead*]

Not hot now. You see?

Mulveroy. I see what?

Pepe. You see? Not hot.

Mulveroy. We haven't got enough vocabulary in common, kid. No exchange of ideas. Nothing gets across.
[*He lies back.*]
All right, you stay and be my water boy. Everybody's got to give up something in this war. Your maman is giving you up.

Ruby.
[*Outside*]
Dat's all right. I got him.
[QUIZZ *enters, followed by* RUBY, *who is carrying* MARION. QUIZZ *arranges blankets to receive him.* PEPE *gets up and helps.*]

Mulveroy. Is he hurt?

Quizz. Just keeled over. Malaria. Hot as a poker.
[*They lay* MARION *down beside* MULVEROY.]

Mulveroy. I got to get up.
[*He tries it and sits down again.*]
Why, God damn it, I can't get up.

Ruby. You stay dere.

Mulveroy. What the hell do you know about that?
[*He sinks back.*]

Ruby. Give me da water.
[PEPE *brings water.* RUBY *bathes* MARION's *forehead.*]

Quizz. Have you ever had this?

Ruby. I got da shakes in 1901. Right here in da Philappines. I still got it. I been eating quinine ever since.
[TATE, SHEVLIN *and* BUSCEMI *enter.*]
He'll be O.K. Just da malaria.—Look. Lay off da gun a minute.

[*They all gather to listen.* RUBY *is squatting beside* MARION.]

We lost da kitchen, see? Ya gotta eat ya iron rations. And we lost da pharmacist and da pharmacist supplies, see? And we lost da lieutenant. And on top a dat we all got malaria.

Tate. All but two of us. Quizz and me. We haven't shivered yet.

Ruby. We all got it, see? Maybe you don't feel it yet, but you all got it, just like Patrick Henry here. And all de quinine's in dis bottle, see? As long as you got quinine you can fight it off, and you can keep going, but you run outa quinine and ya done, see? Now I got da quinine, and da pharmacist's gone, so I give da stuff out. And when I give it out you take it, see? Because if you don't take it ya won't be fit for duty, and if ya ain't fit for duty because ya don't take it dat's malingering.

Quizz. Noboy wants to get out of a duty, Sergeant.

Ruby. On'y I'm telling ya. And anoder ting. We got tree days' iron rations. And maybe two day's quinine. I sent Kriven to the nort' island dis morning wita outrigger. He's gonta make a report how many men left; and da amount of food and quinine. Maybe dey send a boat to take us off. Maybe dey send eats and a nurse. Maybe Kriven never gets dere.—So go easy on ta rations.—Cover da gun for da night. It's too dark to see what ya shooting at.

[TATE, BUSCEMI, SHEVLIN *and* QUIZZ *go out.* RUBY *speaks to* PEPE.]

When he can drink make him swallow dese.

[*He pours a few tablets out of the bottle.*]

Give him water when he wants it, on'y don't drown him.

[PEPE *takes the tablets.* RUBY *follows the men.* PEPE *sits near* MARION *to wait. He moves and then sits up. She offers the gourd.*]

Marion.
> [*In a shaking voice*]
> Cuba Libra?
> [*He tries to take the gourd.*]

Mulveroy. Hold it for him, girl. He's shaking so much he'll knock his God-damn teeth out.
> [MARION *drinks.* MULVEROY *is trying to eat something.*]
> The trouble with my iron rations, they was made of iron.
> [PEPE *slips the tablets into* MARION's *mouth and holds the gourd to his lips again.*]

Marion. You mix your Cuba Libras very bitter, Vision of Delight.

Mulveroy. Swallow it. It's good for you.

Marion. I can't find it.—Battery adjust. Base deflection, right two inches. Converge at focal point. Good, we converge.
> [*His lips make connection with the gourd.* QUIZZ, BUSCEMI *and* TATE *come in, weary, throw themselves down.*]

Quizz. How goes it?

Marion. Whoops!
> [*He spills a little water and gasps.*]
> "How cold are thy baths, Apollo!" I was dreaming. Dull dreams. Classical. I was the young Alexander. Dying, I think. Dying of fever, I think, in the temple of Serapis. I called for, you know, Roxana, and she came, and said I was to go home. "Come home," she said, "it's not necessary to conquer the world. Besides, you have malaria." Then she picked me up to carry me—and I could see that it was not Roxana, it was the Wraith, like a vision of delight. Only I was too heavy and she set me down and offered me something to drink. Then it was Pepe—and we're

twelve thousand miles from St. Cloud. Anyway the Wraith's dancing in New York.

Quizz. In New York?

Marion. She got a dancing job in New York. And she's furnishing an apartment for us.

Quizz. You're dreaming again.

Marion. Am I? That's right. That letter never came. I made that one up. But that other letter—the one she sent from Minneapolis—that was real, wasn't it? You saw that one?

Quizz. Yes, I saw it.

Marion. What did it say?

Quizz. She said when you came home it would all be different. She'd love you and follow you anywhere in the world.

Marion. No, no, I must have dreamed that.

Quizz. No, I read that one. She said she'd follow you anywhere. To the ends of the earth. If only she could see you again.

Marion. Let her follow me here if she meant it. This is the ends of the earth. The last final, ravelled ends.

[SHEVLIN *comes in, puts his rifle away, sits.*]

Mulveroy. Has anybody got a piece of paper? I want to write a letter.

Buscemi. Why should you want to write a letter? With Peppy right here.

Mulveroy. I want to write to me dear old Irish mither on Delancy Street. Living there amongst the Pollacks and the push-carts. Sure, it'll gladden the bitter old heart of her to hear from her wandering son. She niver liked me.

I was born to her old age, be accident, and me arrival was a shame and a calamity to her from the beginning. But I'll write to her anyway. What's the dom date?

[BUSCEMI *hands* MULVEROY *writing materials.*]

Buscemi. Tate has a New England almanac. It tells everything.

[*He starts to write a letter of his own.*]

Tate. Sure.

[*He gets out his almanac.*]

April. Fourth month. Reset fence-posts. Mulch strawberry beds. This is the twenty-fourth. High tide at eight five in the morning, at eight one at night. Yesterday was St. George's day. Tomorrow is St. Mark's. This is the Eve of St. Mark. "Weather, wind, women and fortune change like the moon."

Marion. What pertains to the Eve of St. Mark?

Tate. It's a long story.

[*He reads.*]

"On St. Mark's Eve, if a virgin stand at the church door at dusk she will see entering the church all those of the parish who are to die that year. If her lover should enter among the others he will turn and look at her, may perhaps speak."

Mulveroy. Has to be a virgin or she won't see anything?

Tate. That's right.

Marion. The legend has naturally fallen into disrepute.

Buscemi. Where do I say we are?

Tate. It's a military secret where you are.

Buscemi. Who are we keeping it from? Personally, I'd like to know.

Tate. There's a nest of small rocky islands east of Tawi. We're on one of them. I'm damned if I know which one, and I doubt if it makes much difference.

Quizz. I think I'll borrow a sheet of that paper.
[BUSCEMI *hands it to him.*]

Shevlin. It's not much good writing letters. They'll never get anywhere.

Tate. Why not?

Shevlin. Who's going to take them?

Tate. There was a boat got here yesterday, wasn't there?

Shevlin. What makes you think one'll get through tomorrow?

Tate. We silenced the whole rutting battery on the whole damn rutting spit, didn't we?

Shevlin. They can set up more guns.

Tate. Where're they going to get more guns? The way it looks to me we can send a boat through that channel now and they can't.

Shevlin. I still don't think the postman is going to come around. They don't care how many boats we sink. They'll just keep on sending till we run out of ammunition.

Buscemi. I'd rather be here than on the Jap island. Boy, oh boy, did we make a mess over there today!

Tate. Quizz, where did you learn to shoot a gun?

Quizz. On a farm. There was a lot of luck in where we laid those down. We couldn't see a thing over the crest of the hill, and we just had to guess where they were.

Buscemi. You guessed right.

Marion.
   [*To* Pepe]
   Have you got any more of that stuff?

Pepe. No more.

Quizz. What's the matter?

Marion. Oh, it's coming back. You're all waving around—getting bigger. Go away, Pepe—go away! Oh, God.
   [Pepe *moves around beside* Mulveroy.]

Shevlin. We're all going to be seeing things in a couple of days. This island's rotten with the stuff.

Quizz. Look! Sit down, will you? And talk more to yourself.

Shevlin. What happened to the radio?

Buscemi. Batteries.

Shevlin. What? No program!
   [*He looks at the box.*]
   Jeez, it was at least something when you could get Hollywood on the air! You mean nothing to do but write letters?

Quizz. Oh, the hell with you! I feel good tonight. I know of a lot of Japanese haven't got anything to write home about.

Marion. Quizz?

Quizz. Yes, Francis.

Marion. It's got me again. Everything looks very peculiar—including you.

Tate. Get ready to hold him down, everybody. He's got about a hundred and six.

Quizz. How do I look, boy?

Marion. Give me a drink.
  [Quizz *holds the gourd for him.*]

Tate. He ought to swallow some more quinine. I'll find Ruby.
  [*He goes out right.*]

Marion. You look gigantic. Like a great bat—wavering against the light. Like a huge black king of spades—dancing—Quizz!

Quizz. Yeah?

Marion. I'm sorry. It's nothing.
  [*He looks steadily at a spot where there is nothing visible.*]
  Quizz?

Quizz. Yes?

Marion. Will they laugh at me if I talk to her?

Quizz. Certainly not.

Marion. Because she's here. This is the ends of the earth, and she followed me here.
  [*He looks at the others.*]
  They're all ghostly, like shadows from a fire flickering on the ceiling. And you're a ghost—and Pepe. But the Wraith's as cool and clear as an April morning. Lady sweet, you've been La belle dame sans merci so long, I don't know how to welcome you. She's not really here, Quizz. She smiles at me, but she says nothing. It's just the fever that makes my eyes think they see her.

Quizz. She's as real as I am, boy. As real as any of us.

Marion. It's the fever, and my terrible longing.—There's a
poem we used to say. If she's real she'll answer.

> "Raise the light, my page, that I may see her.—
> Thou art come at last, then, haughty queen!
> Long I've waited, long I've fought my fever:
> Late thou comest, cruel thou hast been."

[*He pauses.*]

You see, she's supposed to speak, and she doesn't.

> "I forgot, thou comest from thy voyage;
> Yes, the spray is on thy cloak and hair.
> But thy dark eyes are not dimmed, proud Iseult!
> And thy beauty never was more fair."

[*He pauses.*]

No, there's no answer.

[*There is a sudden nearby thunder of airplanes. The* Boys
listen, rigid.]

Buscemi. No use going out there. It's too dark to use the
ack-ack.

Quizz. There's a moon, you know. They're probably trying
to drop one on the howitzer.

[*The airplanes are louder. There is an explosion some distance away, to the right.* Quizz *starts out right.*]

Shevlin. Hey, don't be a damn fool.

[*But* Quizz *is gone.* Buscemi *goes to the exit.*]

No use sticking your gourd out.

[*The noise of the planes continues for a few moments. Then
there is a distant detonation and the planes are heard no
more.*]

Buscemi. That last was over the north island.

[Quizz *re-enters.*]

Quizz. They didn't get the gun but they certainly got the
path. Laid one right in the middle of it. There's a hole

thirty feet deep.—Kriven's in with the boat. They must have just missed him.

Shevlin. I'll bet he's shaking in his shoes.

Pepe.
[*To* MULVEROY]

Not good, the water?

Mulveroy. It's getting pretty warm, baby. It could be colder.

Pepe. I get it.
[*She takes the gourds and goes out.*]

Shevlin. Personally, I wouldn't want to be wandering around out there.

Buscemi. They won't come back today.
[KRIVEN *enters with a haversack, which he takes off. He looks about.*]

Kriven. Where's Ruby?

Quizz. I think he went down to his quarters, Sergeant. Tate went looking for him to get some quinine.

Kriven. I got some here.
[*He fishes out a jar.*]

Two hundred tree grain tablets. Who wants it?

Quizz. Marion.

Kriven.
[*Handing the jar to* QUIZZ.]

Feed it to him.
[QUIZZ *administers it.*]

Also, I got about a quarter cord of stinkin' dried fish. And that's all.

Shevlin. We're out of salt.

Kriven. Oh, yeah—and a bag of sea-dust. And the C.O. says we can get the hell out of here any time.

Shevlin and Mulveroy. What's that?

Buscemi. You talked to the C.O.?

Kriven. That's right. And he says we can get the hell out of this island any time.
[*The boys leap to their feet as if with one motion.*]

Mulveroy. Well, by God!
[*He gets up as far as his knees.*]

You hear that, malaria?

Marion. Lord love the C.O.! May he live forever!

Shevlin. When do we start?

Kriven. Any rutting time ya ready.

Mulveroy.
[*To* Quizz]
You hear that, soldier?

Quizz. I never heard anything sounded better.

Kriven. And da C.O. gives me a letter, for Lieutenant Siegel.

Quizz. He was killed this morning, Sergeant.

Kriven. Yeah? Jeez! Well, da letter's got instructions in it, so I better give it to Ruby.
[*He fishes out a note, then pauses.*]
Dere was two men coming down ta path when I came in wit ta outrigger. Dat Jap bomb got bot of dem. Is everybody here but Ruby and Tate?

Shevlin. That's right.

Kriven. Den dat bomb got dem.

> [Quizz *starts out right.*]

You won't find anyting. Just nuttin'.

> [Mulveroy *crosses himself.* Quizz *remains.* Kriven *gives him the note.*]

You read it out loud. I ain't no ruttin' Harvard man.

Quizz.

> [*Reading*]

"Dear Siegel: Considering your reported scarcity of food, quinine and ammunition it appears necessary to evacuate H 23 moving all remaining personnel to H 25, the nearest base where hospitalization is available. The Japs are moving in, and it will not be possible to hold any of this group permanently while Tawi is in their hands. This is not an order, however. Your defense of H 23 and your destruction of batteries and shipping have slowed the enemy considerably. Every day you can hold your position is an incalculable gain. Just for the record let me say that your gunnery has set a high standard, and we're all proud of you. We've seen some of your shells land. If you have to fall back don't think for a moment you haven't done yourselves proud. G. Solway, C.O., H Sector."

Kriven. I don't know wot to hell 'at means, but you better get ya duffle ready so we can start before da sun comes up.

Shevlin. Yes, sir.

> [*They begin to pack up. Nobody speaks for a moment.*]

Quizz. You think we ought to go?

Kriven. What do you tink?

Quizz. I don't know.

Kriven. Look, when ya in a army ya don't have to make it tough for yaself. You can leave dat to da C.O. and da Japs.

Shevlin. We had it tough enough, buddy.

Kriven. You tink we ought ta stay here?

Quizz. I don't know.

Kriven. Listen. Dere was tirty-two men on dis island besides Gooks. Now we down to what's here. Some of us sick and da rest of us going to be sick. Maybe we get off a' here tonight, but if we don't go tonight maybe we never get off here. Da C.O. says dese islands can't be held. He says go ahead an' evacuate. And you want ta stay.

Quizz. No. I want to go home. More than I ever wanted anything in this world. More than I'll ever want anything again. But I don't want to—run out.

Mulveroy. He says, "If you have to fall back don't think you didn't do yourselves proud."

Quizz. I know.

Buscemi. Then for God's sake what's eating you?

Marion. How close does a man have to come to being horizontal before he's earned the right to remain perpendicular?

Shevlin. We've come close enough.

Quizz. It sounded to me as if he was pleading with us—to hold on. If we possibly could.

Marion. There are tens of millions back home who have hardly been touched at all, tens of millions who have risked almost nothing.

Quizz. I know. But they aren't here. And we are.

Kriven. Listen, if you guys want to stick on dis rock we stick, see?

Mulveroy. Mother of God! I thought we was out of here!

Quizz. I'm not deciding it.

Mulveroy. You started it, farmer! Nobody else started it! And now we got to think about it!

Quizz. I'll shut up.
> [*He gets his letter, and sits down.*]

Mulveroy. Maybe we ought to stay, at that. The C.O.'s staying on his ruttin' rock.

Shevlin. Damn it, now you're saying it!

Mulveroy. I'll shut up.
> [*He picks up his letter. There is a general silence.*]

CURTAIN

Act Two

SCENE: *The head of Nell's bed in a circle of light from the oil-lamp that burns beside it.* NELL *is asleep.* QUIZZ's *voice comes from the darkness.*

Quizz.

[*Unseen*]

Mother!

[*There is a long pause.*]

Mother.

[NELL *stirs a little, then is quiet again.*]

Mother.

[NELL *sits up in her bed, listens for a moment.*]

Nell. No. It couldn't be.

Quizz.

[*Unseen*]

Mother.

Nell. Yes. Who is it?

Quizz. It's Quizz.

Nell. You mean—? No, it couldn't be Quizz.

Quizz. Yes.

Nell. You mean you've come home?

Quizz. I had to come and see you.

Nell. Oh, but—I thought—Oh, thank God!

Quizz. Mother—I haven't much time. I want to ask you something.

· 85 ·

Nell. What is it, dear? Come closer, please. I can hardly hear you.

Quizz. Mother, I've come to a place—

Nell. Oh, please come closer.

Quizz. Yes, of course.
[*The light comes up a little on* Quizz, *but still leaves him half in shadow.*]
Is that better?

Nell. Yes.

Quizz. Mother, I've come to a place where we have to choose. It's a question whether we'll let ourselves be driven back—or hang on here. But if we do hang on—I doubt if we'll all live. I doubt if any of us will. And, mother, in the night, one wonders what to do. So I've come to you.

Nell. Isn't there some way—to do what you must—and still come home?

Quizz. Yes. We're not ordered to stay here. It's only—that we're needed, and we know it. And this is what troubles me most. I'm in love, mother. I'm so much in love it's a pain to be away. Every mile away from her was a hurt in my side. And we've never been together. I've never made her mine.

Nell. I know.

Quizz. Oh, mother, I've never taken any woman, because you said I should keep myself pure for my love. So I kept myself for her—and now—if I'm true to myself—it's too late.—Oh, mother, sometimes it seems it's better to stay alive, no matter what guilt you feel—if only you can take your love in your arms again—and lie on her breast—and live. Live a little at least before you die.

Nell. Oh, my son, does it matter about giving up one place to the enemy? It won't matter as much as your lives. It's better to live. If you live now you can fight them again. And we'll see you. We'll see you here again.

Quizz. Should I choose to come home, mother? Oh, don't make it easy for me.

Nell. Must you choose? Doesn't someone choose for you?

Quizz. It seems they'll do as I say. They'll go as I go.
[*A pause*]

Nell. Oh, Quizz! It doesn't matter about the other things! Only come home!
[*The light dims on his face and goes out.*]

Quizz! There's no one. Oh, God, I'm here alone!

CURTAIN

Act Two

SCENE: Janet's bedside, in a ring of light thrown by her oil lamp. JANET *is asleep.* QUIZZ's *voice is heard from the darkness.*

Quizz.

[*Unseen*]

Janet.

Janet.

[*Still asleep*]

Yes, Quizz.

Quizz.

It's so far to you, so far
across time and space and date-lines, yes, sometimes
it seems clear across eternity. Can you hear me?
There as you lie in your bed?

Janet. Yes, sweet.

Quizz.

For me,
here on this hot rock island, it's high noon—
and for you it's midnight. We've let the night go by
and half the day—and still we're not clear in our minds
whether to go or stay.

Janet. Where, darling?

Quizz.

Here,
here on this hot rock island. It's up to us
to hold it—or retreat and save our skins—
and I don't think I'd be tempted to say "Let's go"

if it wasn't for you, there in your midnight bed,
half a world away from me, half a world, and never—
never made mine, never to be mine now
if I cling to my place here.

[*She sits up and looks into the darkness.*]

Janet.

What can it be? I thought—
I thought you spoke to me, Quizz.

Quizz. Yes, I did speak.

Janet. Where are you?

Quizz. Here.

[*The light shows his face.*]

Janet.

Then it's true. You've come home. Oh, darling,
please, never leave me again!

Quizz.

I must ask you something.
Sweet, we had no house. No place and no time,
and it seems to me I'm only a ghost forever
if I should die and you've never been mine in the night,
as if I'd never lived, and left no record—
no son and no name—and another must take my love,
my lost uncompleted love.

Janet.

Oh, darling, I'm yours
or never never anyone's.

Quizz.

The earth
won't have it that way—the dark old plodding earth
says if you're dead you're dead, and a living girl

must mate among the living. So if I die now
I give you to another, and I know that—

Janet.

No, Quizz, never—and you mustn't die!
What makes you speak of dying?

Quizz.

It's noon on this rock
and torrid hot, and six of us who are left
sit in the cave to vote, do we go or stay,
do we make a try for H 25 and home
or man the gun while we can, fire the few shells,
sink the invasion barges, never let them in
till they've paid the last death. And when they come in
be then
the threshold, lie there with this foreign earth;
never with those we love.

Janet.

Who asks this of you?
They shouldn't ask it!

Quizz.

Nobody asks it, dear.
It's something in myself I don't understand
that seems to require it of me. It seems to be
the best of me—the same inner self that turned
to love you and love no one else, that says
give more than is asked of you, be such a man
as she you love could honor at a secret altar
knowing all you've thought and done. But as for orders
we have none now. We're free to go back or stay
save for what's in our minds. And so it seemed
I must talk with you—for you're at the heart of me—
either way it's for you what choice I make—

and I thought it might all come clear if I saw your face
and heard you speak.

Janet.

But you say such terrible things—
that I'd love someone else if you were gone—

Quizz.

Oh, darling,
because I must see what's true and then decide—
because I must look at our dark old plodding earth
the way she is, and then do what I must.
Please, help me see truly!

Janet.

Oh, Quizz, come home!
And oh forgive me, please forgive me now
for knowing so little when you went away,
for letting you leave me, mine and yet not mine—
for I didn't know—but the empty days and nights
have taught me now how if you've missed your love
there's nothing to put in its place.
So you must come home.
Oh, come and find me. Don't leave me empty here.
What could you win worth losing what could be ours?—
What could you win?

Quizz.

Seeing you there in your bed
where I've never lain, it seems that I'd give all heaven
and all the earth, and all men ever had,
to put my arms round you once. You're more beautiful
even
than I remembered.

Janet.

Only for you. Never for anyone else.

Please come home to me here. If you should die
I think I'd die too. And I don't know what to say.
I say the wrong things. But I love you more than you
  know—
more than there's any word for.

Quizz.
  Darling, it doesn't matter,
  anything you say—it's there in your eyes—
  all I wanted to know—and it's here in mine—
  all I could tell you—

Janet.
  Yes—

Quizz.
  And now I must go—

Janet.
  Oh, please—

Quizz.
  Yes, I must.
  It's high noon here on the island,
  and things to do, and voices calling. And so
  God keep you.
    [*The light dims on his face, and goes out.*]

Janet.
  Oh, my darling!—He was here.
  He was here, and he's gone.

CURTAIN

Act Two

SCENE: The cave on the island, indicated as before. MUL-
VEROY *and* MARION *are seated side by side on their pallets
cleaning their guns—which are Springfields or Enfields.*

Marion. Pass me that Hoppe's, if you don't mind.

Mulveroy. You're supposed to boil it, you know. Hoppe's is
strictly against the rules.

Marion. Pass me the Hoppe's, garrulous.
[MULVEROY *hands over the bottle.*]

Mulveroy. I smuggled that bottle out here disguised as Irish
whuskey. Whuskey a sergeant can understand, but pene-
trating oil, that earns a firing squad.
[BUSCEMI *enters with binoculars in his hand.*]

Buscemi. Where's Quizz?

Mulveroy. In there counting cartridges.

Buscemi.
[*Going on through*]
Hey, Quizz! Quizz!

Quizz.
[*Appearing*]
What do you see?

Buscemi. There's a line of barges being towed into the inlet
on the west island. Take a look.

Quizz. Where's the Sergeant?

Buscemi. Coming up.
[QUIZZ *and* BUSCEMI *go out right together.*]

Marion. That's it.

Mulveroy. That's it.—The dirty bastards. Attacking us while we're lying down.

Marion. It's almost enough to spur a man to action.

Mulveroy. A man, yes. These Southern aristocrats, they're a different breed.
[*He climbs up with the aid of his gun.*]
I'm up, anyway. How do I look?

Marion. Suh, your manly features have been ravaged by disease, you lean slightly to the nor-nor-east, and you're more cross-eyed than usual,
[*He begins to rise.*]
but otherwise—

Mulveroy. What are you doing?

Marion. According to my draft board if a man can stand up and see lightning and hear thunder, he can fight.
[*He gets on to his feet.*]

Mulveroy. Lie down, you ruttin' invalid!

Marion. God, you're repulsive. Don't turn that face toward me. Save it for the Japanese!

Mulveroy. Let me be the last to shake your hand.

Marion.
[*Shaking with him*]
Why, certainly. "Morituri salutamus," "The light foot on the sill of shade," and all that sort of stuff. "If I should die think only this of me"—he won't have to look at Mulveroy any more.

Mulveroy. Thanks, pal, thanks. It's an inspiring message.
 [*They turn toward the exit.* QUIZZ *and* KRIVEN *enter.*]

Quizz. If we wait till they begin to come out through the narrows we ought to be able to sink them one at a time. It's a perfect shot for the howitzer.

Kriven. O.K., boy, you take over. My eyes ain't good enough. I can't see 'em wit' ta glasses, even. What ta hell's a' matter wit' you two?

Mulveroy. Don't ask us to bend over, Sergeant, but we can walk around.

Kriven. Get ta hell back on dem blankets!

Marion. Is that an order, sir?

Kriven. No!

Marion. Thank you, sir.
 [BUSCEMI *comes in with* SHEVLIN.]

Shevlin. What are we going to do?

Quizz. We're going to make holes in the bottoms of those barges, as fast as they come out.

Shevlin. We're going to try to hold the island?

Quizz. Wasn't that what we decided last night?

Shevlin. We didn't decide anything last night. We just sat around. Then it looked like it was too late to do anything. But we could still get out of here, you know. We could take the outrigger and cross to H 25 before those barges were anywhere near here.

Kriven. Dat's right. Dat's a trut'.

Buscemi. What do you want to do?

Shevlin. Why don't we take a vote on it?

Quizz. All right. Let's do that. Let's vote on whether we stay on the island one more day. Tomorrow we can take another vote if we feel like it.

Shevlin. If we're still here.

Quizz. Right. If we're still here. Then if there's ever any question what happened—it was a vote. Who's got a pencil?

Buscemi. I don't know why I always furnish the writing materials.

[*He gets paper and pencil, and tears a sheet into strips.*]

Mulveroy. Secret ballot?

Quizz. Secret as you care to keep it. Anybody want to make a speech?

Marion. Yes, I would.

Quizz. Very well, Marion.

Marion. Gentlemen, I find that my natural cynicism is not decreased by tropical malaria and short rations. The apothegms and rebel yells that spring to my lips at this moment are not such as you might expect from one who numbers Patrick Henry among his great-great-grandsires. The emotions that come boiling up out of me are not heroic. I feel myself inclined to mutter something about you're dead a long time, and what do you want, my blood? and if we're offering ourselves up for posterity, who the hell knows if he'd like posterity, and what difference does it make about one rock in a whole ocean, and listen, fellows, we won't get another chance back there among the women we love and the cold drinks and the things we want to do. Who the hell picked us out to save the world, anyway? And are we perfectly sure it's worth the effort? And what's the good of saving the whole world if you happen to die in the process? But I vote to try it another day.

Buscemi. What?

Marion. I vote to try it another day, and probably another day after that.

Buscemi. Why in hell do you do that?

Marion. Because man is not a reasonable creature. Because I'm essentially a fool like those rutting ancestors of mine. —And, you know, I want to sink those God damn Jap boats. I want to sink all of them. I only hope you have more sense than I have. Here's my vote.

    [*He writes it, places it in a helmet.* Quizz *passes the helmet around. They all vote silently.*]

Quizz. Shall I count them?

Kriven. Go ahead.

    [Quizz *looks at the six votes.*]

Quizz. There's something wrong here. Everybody votes aye. Everybody votes to stay.

Shevlin. What's the matter with that?

Quizz. You voted to stay?

Shevlin. Sure I voted to stay.

Quizz. Attaboy.

    [*A bomber is heard outside. Then a crash.* Quizz *looks out.*]

They missed the gun. They just can't seem to locate that gun. And there's a string of barges coming toward the point. It's our move.

Kriven. Positions!

[*They all run out.* KRIVEN *is heard outside giving commands.*]

Aiming point—dat first boat. You take it, Quizz. I can't see ta damn ting!

Quizz.

[*Outside*]

Target, that first boat, deflection one zero, fire as the boats come out! Fire!

[*The howitzer is heard. Once, twice, three times.*]

CURTAIN

Act Two

SCENE: The kitchen of the farm as it was in the first act except for a small radio on the table. DECK *and* NELL *are seated listening.*

The Radio. "It is quite possible that the Philippines have not been entirely abandoned by American forces. In those numberless islands there are many natural fastnesses, well equipped for defense, difficult to attack. Mopping up operations may take many months—and may never be completed. How many American soldiers still hold out in that wilderness of atolls and volcanic peaks is, of course, a military secret, but even if it were not, there is nobody either in Washington or elsewhere who knows all the facts as of today."

Nell.

[*Switching off the radio.*]

I guess we can do without the rest. He doesn't know any more than we do, and he admits it.

Deck. I guess I hang around the house a good deal, listening to that thing.

Nell. I thought you were waiting for a call from Neil and Zip. They really should be on the afternoon train.

Deck. It'll be kind of a welcome change around here with those two banging doors, and sliding to every stop.

Nell. The two extra plates on the table look mighty good to me.

Deck. Think I ought to drive over to the train anyway—even if they don't call?

Nell. No. don't worry about them. That's what they don't like. If you met the train they'd likely arrive while you were gone—driving over from Alfred with somebody.

Deck. Right you are, girl. I'll be getting back to work.
 [*He rises*]
Damn it, "missing" can mean so many things. Every once in a while I stop short in the field and think of another one.

Nell. I do it, too.

Deck. Ralph's out there waiting for me. It must be close to three.
 [*He looks at his watch*]

Nell. I set the clock back yesterday. It keeps running away ahead into tomorrow, that clock.

Deck. By God, if I was a clock I'd be pushing day after to-morrow all the time.
 [*Casually*]
Did you read in the paper, about the fellows landing in Australia, all the way from Corregidor in an open boat?

Nell. I never miss anything like that, dear. Those things jump right out of the page at me.

Deck.
 [*At the door*]
I guess Ralph'll wait a few minutes.

Nell. Somebody coming?

Deck. Feller's dropping Janet at the gate.

Nell. The mail was late today.
 [*There is a silence.* JANET *appears at the door.*]

Janet. Oh, mother, mother—there's a letter!

Nell. Not from Quizz?

Janet. Yes, from Quizz!

Deck. Good news?

Janet. I've only just looked inside. I didn't dare read it alone. It came in an army envelope, and there's a note from his captain—but there's a letter from Quizz too.

Nell. Oh.

Janet. It's his writing—some of it.

> [*She offers the envelope to* NELL, *who takes out the letters and holds them in her hand for a second, but makes no attempt to decipher them before handing them to* JANET.]

Nell. I guess you'll have to read them.

Deck. You've got the young eyes, Janet.

Janet. All right.

> [*She reads*]

"Dear Miss Feller. You have of course been notified that Private West is listed as missing. H 23, the island on which he was stationed, was captured by the Japanese about two months ago. It is impossible to report definitely concerning our men who were on the island, but it is supposed that some are prisoners. They acted with extraordinary courage and effectiveness and we hope they all turn up later to receive the medals they have coming to them. I am writing you now to enclose some fragments of a letter delivered to me, along with other messages and letters, by a Filipino girl who escaped from H 23 in an outrigger canoe. I have only recently reached a point within our own lines where I could sort the papers and mail them. Unfortunately only a few pages of your letter reached me. Sincerely yours, Captain G. Solvay."

Then—here are the pieces of his letter:

"April 29th. Dear, I haven't written you for two days. It seems I had malaria pretty bad and didn't know what was going on. Today I'm a little shaky but I'm up. Sergeant Kriven died in the night, and I'm the only excuse for an officer there is around here. The Japs are certainly determined to blow us out of this place. This gun of ours covers the north and south channel through the islands and we're holding up a lot of . . ."

That's all of that page—and then, there's one more little piece:

"Some nights I try to think myself clear out of this place, and round the world to you, and once or twice I seemed to be there in your room, but I'm never sure I found you. And now I can only say, all my love, Quizz."

[*She looks up.*]

Deck. Is that all?

Janet. Yes.

Deck.

[*Rising*]

I know what I'm going to think. He's alive, and he's well, and he'll come through and get home.

Nell. That's what I believe.

Janet.

[*But not so certainly*]

Yes.

Deck. And I know what I'm going to do. There's only one thing for a man to do nowadays—and that's go out and enlist.

Nell. Enlist?

Deck. And I don't care what in! Any armed service where I can get a chance to fight.—That's what I want! That's what I've wanted to do all along—and now I'm going to do it!

Nell. Do you think—?

Deck. What?
 [*She doesn't answer, begins instead to finish setting the table.*]

Nell. Maybe we're more good here on the farm, Deck, both of us.

Deck.
 [*His hands on her shoulders*]
 Look, Nell—I'm sick of the farm. I feel as if I was running away from them here on the farm. I'm going into Olean to see about it.

Nell. Don't hold me, Deck. Let me walk up and down my kitchen, and carry things the way I always do. It's the only way I know to keep going. Don't hold me.
 [*He lets her go. She carries the dishes to the table.*]
 It's better to keep on with the same things. You're doing better here than you could in any armed service.

Deck.
 [*Afraid of breaking down*]
 Ralph's waiting for me. I'll go start the machinery.
 [*He goes out.*]

Nell. It's worse for you than for us, Janet. Don't think we don't know.

Janet. Let me help you.
 [*She gets up.*]

Nell. You don't need to.

Janet. I want to help you.
> [*She carries some dishes.*]

Do you think he'll come back?

Nell. I don't know, Janet. I guess we just hope so.

Janet. Because I—I can't think so. In my mind. Can you?

Nell. Why do you ask me?

Janet. Did you ever have a feeling that he was near you in the night?

Nell. Yes, more than once.

Janet. I suppose one imagines.—But that's why I think I won't see him again. It's—as if he told me. They made a decision that meant they wouldn't come home.

Nell. A decision?

Janet. Yes.

Nell. Could it be that we have the same dreams?

Janet. Did you have it, too?
> [*She takes Nell's hand.*]

Nell. Wait.—It's shadowy now, the way dreams are in the daytime. But for a moment.—No, it's gone.

Janet. I suppose it was dreams. But the last time it was so real I could have touched him—so real I can remember words he said.

Nell. What did he say?

Janet. He said, "Those who love you can't tell you what you must do. They can only say, save yourself. If they love you they can't say anything else. But the soldier, there with his comrades, and with the enemy in front of him, he must decide for himself." That's why I think he won't come home.

Nell. Janet, darling, you've been carrying this with you, all these weeks!

Janet. But something happened between us that last night—that gave me a way to live. He said, "Don't think it's all loss. There's a kind of glory between us we couldn't have had. We eat our iron rations at a secret altar." It's—as if it was our marriage.

Nell. He must have loved you terribly, for his words reach you clear round the earth.

Janet. I love him terribly. But—if they'd left the island they'd have been defeated—in their own hearts—and when they stayed there—that was a victory. I wouldn't want him to be defeated. We can't decide for them because we love them.

Nell. He's yours now forever, darling. He was mine for a little while, but you'll have him always, even if he doesn't come back.
[DECK *comes in followed by* RALPH.]

Deck. Happened to remember about that news broadcast, so if you girls won't laugh at me I'll just turn it on.
[*He tunes the radio.*]

Nell. How's the mowing?

Ralph. Just starting on the cemetery meadow, Nell. It's a good stand. High and heavy.
[*The radio speaks.*]

The Radio. "Have you noticed that our soldiers almost never talk about the war, almost never discuss our reasons for fighting? I've noticed it. And have you wondered why? I think I know. This is the first war in history where there's no possible argument about who's right and who's wrong.

We're fighting for our lives and fighting to keep men free. You can't argue about that. You don't need any oratory to convince people, nor songs to keep up their spirits in such a war. And so it's a war without oratory and without songs —because we know very well what we're doing."

[Cy *comes to the door, stands for a moment without speaking.*]

Ralph. Something on your mind, Cy?

Cy. You know, Zip got out of a car down at the corners, and he's walking up the road, and there's a soldier coming with him.

[*He pauses.*]

A soldier looks like Quizz.

Deck. Like Quizz?

Cy. I swear to God—it looks like Quizz!

[Deck *gets up from the radio, and goes to the door. After a moment he steps back from it across the room.* Nell *and* Janet *have risen.* Neil *comes in wearing a uniform, followed by* Zip]

Deck. What's this mean?

Neil. It's mine, dad.

Deck. No wonder he said you looked like—

Nell. Oh, Neil, Neil!

Neil. I know I should have said something first, but I was afraid you'd say no.

Deck. I guess we would have.

Nell. Oh, Neil! You could have waited till later. Till you were called.

Neil. No, I couldn't mother.

Zip. And I can't, either.

Nell. You, Zip? What do you mean?

Zip. They wouldn't take Neil in the air force because of his eyes. So he joined the artillery. But they'll take me.

Deck. You've signed up for a pilot?

Zip. I have to get your permission.

Nell. If it had come a little later. Today—Janet has a letter from Quizz. We don't know whether he'll come back. It's sort of a last letter—

Neil. That's why we had to go, mother. That's why we couldn't wait. Because of Quizz. It's what Quizz would want us to do.

Deck. How do you know that?

Neil. I don't know. But it's as if I could hear him saying it. We couldn't stay here on the farm, and know he'd left something unfinished out there. We had to take it up— and carry it on.

Zip. I'm the age they want, mother. For the air force. And if I'm old enough to fight, I'm old enough to make up my mind.

Neil. As a matter of fact I haven't been at the U. for a couple of months. Zip's been kind of covering for me. I didn't write because it seemed better to talk about it, mother.

Nell. Yes.

Neil. And, dad, it seemed wrong, when there was only one important thing to do in the world, to look the other way, and let somebody else do it. I know you thought I was coming back to the farm, and I know they need farm workers, but—tell the truth I want to get out there where the fight's going on. Suppose they make the world over, more the way it ought to be, and everybody has a better chance—well, I want to pay for my ticket.

Deck. I suppose it might turn out better.

Neil. Anyway, if it isn't I don't want it to be my fault.

Zip. That's right.

Deck. Mother, what can we do with these two? What can we do?

Nell. What can we do, Janet?

Janet. I guess Quizz would say—we had to let them go.

Deck. Maybe I'm just holding back from being old, but they look mighty young to me. I'd rather go myself.

Ralph. The army don't want us any more, Deck. I tried it.

Deck. You tried it?

Ralph. I went down and tried to enlist. But they want these young fellows. They're the men of the house now. They're the fighting men.

Nell.

[*Going over to Deck*]

And it's true we can't hold them back because we love them. Every man has to follow his own vision. That's the way new world's are made.

Deck. All right, boys. You go out and make things over your way. We old folks, we'll stay here, damn it, and milk the cows and run the baler.

[NEIL *and* ZIP *cross to kiss* NELL.]

Make a new world, boys. God knows we need it.

CURTAIN